Contents

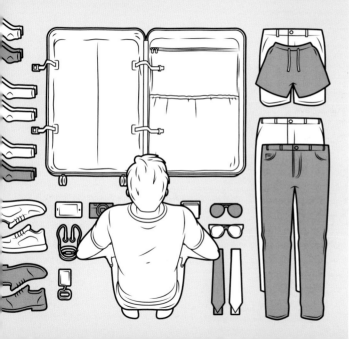

- Contents -

Introduction

An art, a science, a necessary evil: packing is a task all travellers must tackle before their journey even begins. Not many of us, however, do it well, and even fewer of us approach it with any sense of pleasure. Let us fix that. Step away from that mountainous pile of clothing, get up off that suitcase you're trying to squash shut, and allow this book to unclutter your path to luggage liberation.

Do you tip the scales into excess charges every time the family holidays, or are you a frugal carry-on-only business traveller looking for even smarter ways to minimise? Do you need savvy kit suggestions for your next foray into the wilderness or are you a luxury island hopper wanting the best couture on the move?

Whatever your style, we hope this neatly arranged book will help you keep your luggage equally on message and well organised. Take the pain out of packing by using our cut-out-and-keep lists. Teach the kids to pack and learn how to edit your own capsule wardrobe. Take comfort and inspiration in stories of packing mishaps and luggage pioneers from days gone by. Or simply drool over the latest must-have hard-shell, hi-tech spinner or re-imagined retro steamer case.

Packing light is once again à la mode. As the author Antoine de

Saint-Exupéry once said: 'He who would travel happily, must travel light.' When it comes to your suitcase, less really is more, leaving you light on your feet and free to immerse yourself in local culture and nature without being weighed down by masses of kit.

However, packing light also takes more time, more strategy and potentially a lot more faffing around. Happily, it is a skill that can be learned. And when less is not necessarily more (we're looking at you, yoghurt-coated, rice-cracker-splattered 'holidaying' parents), we can help you decide what, how and when to pack for tantrum-free travels.

Whatever type of traveller you are, we can up your packing game. Learn how to make your tech work harder and choose apps that will pack for you. Are you a weekender, a business traveller or an adrenaline junkie? Our aim is to matchmake your luggage to your travel type, and find a suitcase (backpack, wheelie or duffel) that's a true soulmate, in it for the long haul. It matters not if you're going round the world for a year or taking a cheeky city break, we have definitive packing lists, tailor-made tips and life hacks for all.

As organisational guru Marie Kondo says: 'A messy room equals a messy mind.' The same goes for your suitcase. Happy packing!

How to be a packing maestro

Luggage: evolution

Luggage has come a long way over the centuries – from the animal-hide holdalls of the Middle Ages to the plastic ride-on cases sported by kids in airports today. Modern suitcases, born out of hefty trunks of wood with iron frames, saw their evolution leap forwards with the arrival of steamships. Waterproofed with canvas or tree sap, these chunky clunkies were the height of technology.

1153: The first wheeled luggage rolls into existence during the Crusades, when the Knights Templar use it to carry arms, chain mail and shoe-mending tools.

1596: The term 'luggage' is coined, from the Middle-English word 'lug' meaning 'to drag'.

1870: Louis Vuitton debuts a flat-top 'steamer trunk' designed to stack easily on ships: the prototype for the modern suitcase is born.

1910: The Shwayder Trunk Manufacturing Company launches with the tagline 'strong enough to stand on'. Later (in 1966) to become Samsonite, it pioneers the hard-shell case.

1920s–'50s: The evolution of mass transportation sees a boom in luggage design. There's now a case for every occasion and item, from cameras and dresses to cigars and hats.

The suitcase spans every transportation revolution, from steamer to passenger jet. With the late 19th century came mass tourism and, a handful of decades later, mass aviation. Today, luggage design is intricately linked to aircraft, from practical demands of baggage handling to what can squeeze into that overhead locker. In their myriad designs, our cases carry not just our stuff but also a history of human movement.

1972: **A US company patents suitcases with wheels.**

1987: **Pilot Bob Plath invents Rollaboard® luggage, a vertical rather than horizontal suitcase with wheels that can easily be towed through airports and stowed on planes; the granddaddy of today's wheelie cases.**

1994: **The telescopic/ collapsible handle is invented and patented by Don Ku.**

2006: **British company Trunki launches and soon dominates the world of family-friendly luggage with its ride-on suitcases.**

2014: **Luggage with GPS tracking capabilities becomes available.**

The grand tourist
If you were young, titled and adventurous in the 18th century, it's likely you'd go on a 'grand tour'. These early European road trips took in the exotic arts and culture of the Continent, lasted many months and were supported by a cavalcade of hired hands carrying trunks and furniture by ship, train and donkey. Packing took nearly as long as the trips themselves, with guidebooks of the time recommending travellers carry such essentials as a medicine chest, a 'necessaire' of cutlery (travellers were expected to bring their own) and toiletries, along with weapons (for servants) to fend off bandits, and bedbug-proof leather sheets. Generally, an entire carriage was devoted to baggage. However, as mass transport improved, tourism was no longer solely the preserve of the horse-drawn upper classes and the 'grand' element faded into history.

Plastic fantastic

Early suitcases might have been more portable than wooden trunks but they were far from lightweight, being made from leather, wicker or rubber cloth with brass-capped corners. As cars became popular in the 1930s, they reduced the need for heavy-duty baggage: metal clasps eventually gave way to zips, and leather to plastic. Today's suitcase is largely made out of synthetic fabric stretched over a light alloy frame.

> 'We'll have no trunks. Only a carpet bag, with two shirts and three pairs of stockings for me, and the same for you. We'll buy our clothes on the way.'
>
> Phileas Fogg in Around the World in Eighty Days (the 1873 novel by Jules Verne).

Luggage: selection

*Are you a spinner or a backpacker? The type of trip you're taking
and how you're getting there will inform your choice of luggage.*

The spinner
There's none so chic as those who
glide through the terminal with a
sleek, shiny spinner at their side.
We can only guess at the tastefully
collated glamour packed within.

The weekender
When there's little substance, you
can afford more style — after all, a
capacious bag is just the right size
for that carefully selected capsule
weekend wardrobe.

The business traveller
You're so good to go with a
compact, accessible Tardis.
Laptop and paperwork,
check. Change of shirt and
underwear, check.

Tag and go
Spotting your bags on the
luggage belt can present a
challenge. Some might opt for
a brightly coloured case. But if
you're a little more 50 shades
of grey, consider a subtle yet
eye-catching luggage tag.
Even Tiffany & Co. offers a
stylish leather number in its
signature teal.

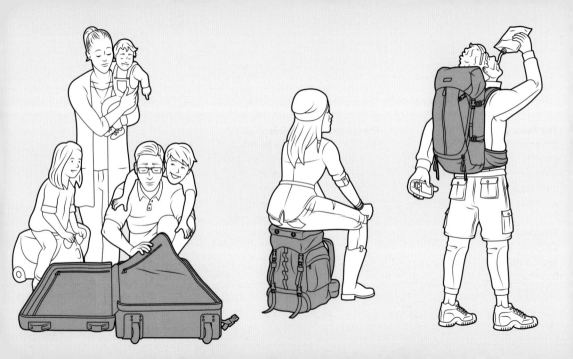

The family
When you're blessed with 2.4 children, a double-sided suitcase is the only way to keep family affairs in order. For the .4, a Trunki – what else?

The backpacker
Q. When is a backpack a handy seat? A. When it's a killer to carry. But it's all in there. Oh yes, it's all in there.

The adrenaline junkie
Mistake the adventurer for the backpacker at your peril. This man will drill holes in the handle of a toothbrush to shed weight – and he's had that hip belt specially heat-treated to mould to his body, don't you know.

It's a wrap
Some might say it's a shocking use of plastic, but if you can't bear your bags getting bumped and bruised, consider shrink-wrapping – it'll keep your belongings safe as well as preserve the bag's good looks. Downside? You could probably buy a whole new set of luggage with the money you spend on it.

Luggage: key features
Stop, look, listen. Size, colour, two wheels or four – there is much to consider when buying luggage.

False economy
You get what you pay for. Spend a little more for better design and baggage that uses the latest materials, quality components and comes with a guarantee against bits falling apart. You'll also get little extras, such as integrated luggage labels and TSA locks. Expect a decent case to last for 10 years.

Size matters
You can now buy luggage built to the size specifications of different airlines. Consider an expandable case for ultimate versatility; it's ideal for trips lasting from two days to two weeks.

Hard or soft
A hard shell is great for protecting your possessions but loses points for dead weight and inflexibility. Soft-sided luggage can deal with a squash and a squeeze but can be vulnerable to rips.

Pretty in pink
Think carefully before you're seduced by that case in a pastel

Did you know...
The luggage belts in the old baggage reclaim at Cork Airport in Ireland used to trundle around tropical aquariums. These splendid displays were designed to resemble the marine landscapes of Lake Tanganyika and the Amazon River.

shade because it won't look smart for long – there's a reason why most of us opt for darker colours.

Two wheels bad

The traveller with a drag-along in a busy airport is about as popular as cholera. The two-wheeler will take its toll on your back, arms and shoulders, too. Check out a four-wheel spinner – even four double wheels – which will simply glide alongside you. Delsey has added a handbrake to its collection.

Hold on tight

Go for a pop-up handle; some are also adjustable for those on the short or tall side. Smart backpacks convert to wheelie bags for when you don't want to carry the world on your shoulders.

A place for everything

Zipped side pockets, zip-off pockets, mesh divider pads, elastic cross ribbons, laundry bags, suit compartments… Which of these could prove really useful for your style of travelling?

Luggage:
deluxe design

Once upon a time, to travel was to make a statement of wealth. But in the age of mass air transit, it's often your luggage that lets the world know your VIP credentials.

 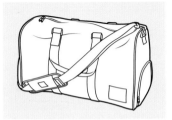

For the blue blood:
Swaine Adeney Brigg

Purveyors to both Prince Charles and his mum, Swaine Adeney Brigg's Windsor Handmade Leather Luggage Set is made from bridle leather and finished with brass locks, and is individually tailored for every client.

For the dapper explorer:
Globe-Trotter

Handcrafting bags for the likes of Sir Edmund Hillary for more than 100 years, Globe-Trotter's recently launched the SPECTRE collection with black leather tooled by vintage Victorian machinery – for those wannabe Bonds out there.

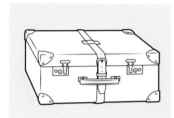 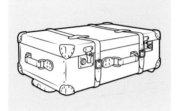 

For the alpha traveller: Tumi

The ultimate combination of tough-wearing technology and luxurious design, Tumi's Alpha range comes with a 4 Wheeled Extended Trip Garment Bag that will set you back as much as a business-class ticket to New York.

For the European socialite: Hermès

The French fashion house has been making braggish bags for the design-conscious since 1837. Leather has never looked better, cut into understated styles, brazen with bold colours. This is the prettiest investment you'll ever make.

For the heritage backpacker: Herschel

Created in 2009, Herschel's 'heritage' brand is made up of folksy packs with straps and buckles befitting a gold-rush miner, but with all the functionality of the finest, contemporary-designed travel kit.

‹ For speed demons: Valextra
Want your luggage to streak
ahead of the pack? Go for the
Avietta Luggage Set by Valextra.
Its wheeled cases are pimped with
Pirelli wheels.

**› For protective
owners: Samsonite**
The hard-shell pioneers have been
making indestructible bags for
more than a century and lay
claim to creating the strongest,
lightest bag yet: the Cosmolite.
Crafted from distinctive, ribbed
Curv® material, this bag is both
fashion-forward and seriously on
the defensive.

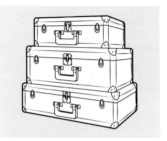

^ For the jet set: Louis Vuitton
Favoured by the Grand Travellers
of the 1800s, you can still buy
Vuitton's classic leather range:
a wardrobe, steamer trunks, an
armoire and accessories, trolleys
and cases. Probably the most
expensive luggage set out there.

21

Luggage: technology

Come the revolution, we'll all have smart luggage. Biometric locking, global tracking, phone charging – these are just some of the tricks you'll soon be able to expect your suitcase to perform.

Samsonite is hard at work with Samsung on a new futuristic collection of suitcases with embedded technology that will be managed from an app. Built-in GPS locators will enable you to track your case and even alert you if someone tries to tamper with it. This luggage will be so smart it will be able to turn itself off while in flight to keep the security folk happy.

Suitcases that follow you around could soon be a reality in airport terminals - and even a bag that will check itself in is in development. Again, Samsonite and Samsung are at the forefront of the race to make it possible for built-in chips to tag a bag remotely. The promise of improved check-in efficiency means some of the major airlines are involved in the project.

Yet it is a startup that has beaten the big boys to getting the first smart case on to the luggage conveyor belts. Bluesmart, a hand-luggage-sized suitcase, is now being shipped to customers. The lightweight hard case features GPS tracking and a battery so powerful it claims to be able to charge a mobile phone up to six times. Customer feedback on public review sites reveals varying degrees of satisfaction.

Like all pioneering technology, expect prices for smart luggage to be high for a while – and us to all take this technology for granted by the end of the next decade.

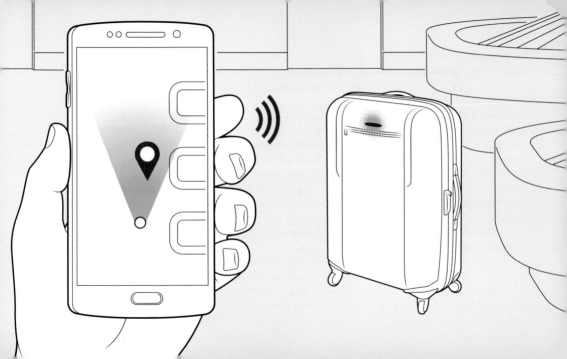

Luggage: clever kit
Over the baggage allowance? Phone run out of juice?
Here are some nifty designs to cut out common travel problems.

Weigh-to-fly
Is it a scale, is it a tracker, is it a hanger? Weigh-to-fly is all three. The extendable digital device performs several functions via its app. It will weigh your luggage without you having to lift it up (you can even program different airlines' limits); the proximity sensor will detect if you've wandered away from your case and alert you; and the design means it can double as a clothes hanger. *weigh-to-f.ly*

Crumpled City
Coming soon to a metropolis near (or far from) you is the waterproof, tear-resistant cloth map you can screw up and stuff in your pocket. Currently, Crumpled City covers more than 40 conurbations, focusing on large parts of each city, with an index of attractions and insider tips. Just take care not to leave it on a restaurant table for the waiter to sweep up with the napkins… *pizzolorusso.com*

Foutala
The towel that thinks it's a shawl. Or is it the shawl that thinks it's a towel? Either way, these covetable 100% cotton, tassle-edged wraps come in a variety of pastels and bolds, with stripes as thick or thin as you like. Lightweight yet absorbent, they are beloved by yachties and beach bums. *foutala.com*

Vacuum bags
These little suckers, well, suck up your possessions in a neat

compressed bundle that can take up three-quarters less space than the unsquashed pile of stuff. They come in various sizes and, if you don't have a vacuum cleaner handy, you can just roll out the excess air.

Wolffepack

This orbital backpack has thrown the cards in the air for the luggage industry. Stick the Wolffepack on your back and, when you need to dip inside, just pull a cord. By sleight of design (and many magnets), hey presto, the main body of the bag will swing round to the front for easy delving. *wolffepack.com*

Solarmonkey Adventurer Powertraveller

Who needs an electric socket when you can power your devices with the sun? Solarmonkey Adventurer Powertraveller is every traveller's energetic friend and it's water- and shock-resistant, too. *powertraveller.com*

Noise-cancelling headphones

Not only will a pair of these small but seriously useful 'phones guarantee you stay friends with your fellow travellers, but they can also seriously cut down engine noise on aircraft. Aim high (in price); Bose is highly recommended.

USB cable and battery pack

Keep a USB cable handy – many new planes now have sockets for these plugs, even if you're sitting in the back of the bus. If your plane still has the comforts of a Lancaster bomber, a USB battery pack is a lifesaver.

Rise

Check out the nifty bags with shelves from Rise. Its selection of luggage has integrated soft shelving that lifts out to hang on a rail or the back of a door. You can buy inserts to pack in your existing luggage, too. We're sold. *www.risegear.com*

Ostrich Pillow

Style or substance, our jury's out on the Ostrich Pillow. You'll certainly turn heads if you sport this cosy cocoon (see left) and you're highly likely to doze off, too. *www.ostrichpillow.com*

Pack 'appy
Three apps that (almost) do the packing for you.

Travel List
One for the analogue traveller: this is the closest thing to Post-It notes, pen and paper and as minimalist as they come. Create your packing lists, tick off items and the app only shows you what's left. If you like life, and luggage, uncluttered and simple, this may be the list for you. You can customise the app to give you alerts and reminders. IOS/ GooglePlay

TripList
An interactive list that caters for all types of travel, be it business or pleasure, beach or city. It has categories for different types of clothing and a 'task' list. Items are pleasingly ticked off once packed (but still visible in a 'checked items' list). It also offers useful peripheral support, such as alerts for upcoming travel dates and deadlines, plus a way to source things you might have forgotten. IOS

Packing Pro
Organise all your essentials by category, then check them off as you go. True list lovers can indulge by making lists within a list, and everything can be customised. The initial set-up might take some getting used to (some say it's fussy), but once the basic templates are organised, this app is perfect for those who travel frequently or who have to corral luggage for a large family. IOS

Packing: are you an overpacker or an underpacker?
What do you need for a three-night break in Lisbon? Possibly not what you have packed in your bag...

The Overpacker:
Weighing in at 10kg

Clothing: 4 x boxers and socks; 2 x shorts; trousers; gym shorts and 2 x gym T-shirts; swimming trunks; 3 x polo shirts; 3 x T-shirts; vest; hoodie; fleece; trainers; jacket.

Toiletries: transparent bag of 100mL potions and pastes.

Tech: 7in tablet; iPod; Bluetooth speaker; 2 x adaptors; 3 x chargers;

> I could have lived for up to a week with what I'd packed. I was covered for every eventuality, weather-wise. '

mobile phone; earphones; bridge camera; compact camera.

Miscellaneous: 2 x newspapers; wallet; 2 x coin purses; keys; sunglasses; daypack; 2 x pens.

Didn't wear/use: gym shorts; swimming trunks; 1 x gym T-shirt; 2 x polo shirts; trousers; shorts; 1 x socks; 1 x pants; fleece; daypack.

Favourite luxury item:
Bluetooth speaker.

With hindsight, wouldn't have packed: 1 x polo; fleece.

Returned with purchase:
Trainers; earphones.

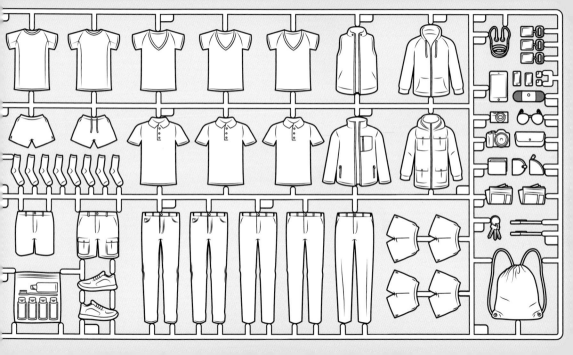

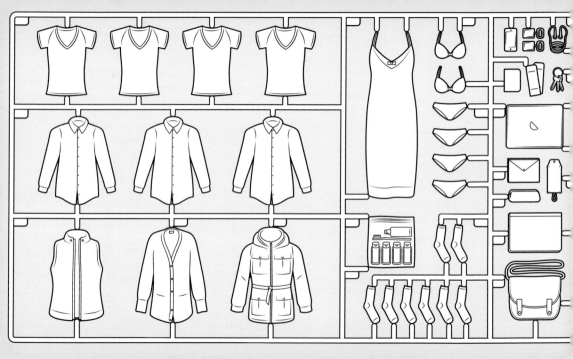

The Underpacker
Weighing in at 6kg

Clothing: 2 x bras; 4 x knickers and socks; nightie; 4 x T-shirts; vest top; 3 x blouses; cardigan; waterproof jacket.

Toiletries: transparent bag of 100mL potions and pastes.

Tech: 15in laptop; phone and laptop chargers; adaptor; earphones.

Miscellaneous: purse; keys; fold-up bag; mobile phone; passports and boarding cards; notebook; pencil case; keys.

Didn't wear/use: 2 x blouses; 1 x knickers; 1 x socks; cardigan; foundation pen; hair gel; fold-up bag; earphones.

Favourite luxury item: laptop.

With hindsight, wouldn't have packed: hair gel.

Returned with purchase: new jacket.

'I used to pack really light, but experience has taught me to pack more, to give myself more choice. I felt I needed a second pair of trousers and a more versatile jacket – which is why I bought one. I also wish I'd packed a second pair of shoes. I ended up carrying my partner's new trainers home in my luggage!'

Packing: list-making

*Even the savviest wanderer
uses a list. What type? Well,
that depends on who you are
and where you're going.*

He's been everywhere, he's seen
everything. What use has the smug
traveller for a list? But a reminder,
well, that's different. Isn't it?

Proper prior preparation prevents
poor performance. For some,
packing is a challenge that begins
two weeks before departure
with a brainstorm to cover every
eventuality. Next comes the edit,
where order is imposed, with
careful categorisation. And finally,
the definitive list is born.

An editable checklist is a lifesaver for parents packing for the family. And it can be updated at the click of a mouse. (The kids might even help compile it.) Then it can be used to ensure that everything is packed for the schlep home - so that you don't leave that all-important teddy behind.

Make an art of what most would deem to be a tiresome task. The holiday for this daydreamer starts from the moment pen is put to Moleskine®. These inventories are lovingly curated – with illustrative flourishes – for different types, even lengths, of holiday. This is less a list, more a travel journal.

Be ready for action
When is a list not a list? When it's a Mother Bag. Keep your core kit ready to go – a toiletry bag that is never decanted, travel adaptor, sarong, eye mask and ear-plugs, shoe and laundry bags. Some keep these essentials in their luggage, others dedicate a whole drawer to them.

Packing: the philosophy of packing light

Mindfulness and minimalism: ubiquitous modern buzzwords. But the liberation of decluttering is magical. Travel light, learn to simply 'be'... and get more from the world in return.

Layer for enlightenment

Accommodate different climates and looks from one outfit by packing clothes that can be layered. Function and fashion taken care of, you can forget what's on the outside and concentrate on what's within.

Be fluid, be solid

Liquids weigh you down – and slow you down at airport security.

> 'When you figure out your suitcase, you figure out your life.'
>
> *Fashion designer Diane von Furstenberg.*

Decant toiletries into small bottles and use solid alternatives wherever possible. See page 47 for tips.

Clean clothes, clear mind

Choose fabrics that wash and dry easily, then simply cleanse the contents of your suitcase (and thus your soul) as required on the go.

Purge your suitcase

Pile all your clothing on the floor. You may be travelling across mountains, but you do not need to pack one. Systematically remove at least a third of your items.

Packing: stylist tips

Rather die than be seen in a pair of zip-off trouser-shorts? Don't worry, there's plenty of space for style in your luggage if you follow these expert tips from Gemma Hayward, Senior Fashion Editor at Grazia.

Set out different outfits for your needs. Start with key pieces, such as a pair of denim shorts, and select a number of tops to go with them. Then work out how many more days you need options for and include outfits to suit different activities.

Separate the day and night garments and work on creating full looks, including accessories. If you have a clear idea of your schedule and your destination, this should be really easy to do.

Generally, I get my clothes ready a week before – a dream collection with far too many looks put together and a different pair of shoes for every day. Then, I go back to it a couple of days later, look at everything and edit down.

I find I am more critical on the second viewing and can get rid of things that I don't think I will need or have gone off. This way, only the items I really want to wear will make it into the case.

It's a system that works really

well for me. I have managed to travel surprisingly light on my past few trips, returning home with hardly anything clean. Accessories are my downfall. I don't seem to be able to go on holiday without at least three pairs of sunglasses.

Don't leave home without…

Blazer
This classic wardrobe staple looks cool with a T-shirt and sneakers, yet will make a classic shirt and jeans evening-ready.

Flat shoes or trainers
Pointy pumps, ballet flats, Birkenstocks or skate trainers – anything goes, so long as they're neutral in colour and not something you'd wear to the gym.

Shirt
Oversized shirts look chic when teamed with a skinny silhouette on the bottom half, but are equally stylish over swimwear at the beach.

Dark denim jeans
Opt for a darker wash. That way, you can also wear them in the evening for a smarter look.

Heels
You might not need them, but it's always good to have some just in case. They can be the catalyst for outfit transformation.

Plain white T-shirt
Yes, a little boring, but it's the key to layering. It'll sit nicely under that shirt or blazer. If it's crisp white, it'll work well on its own for both smart and casual occasions.

Flip-flops
The times I have taken five pairs of fancy sandals and only worn Havaianas the entire time…

Get the look
For beach bums: Heidi Klein
For country living: Barbour
For sailors: J.Crew
For safari: Hickman & Bousfield
For skiers: Arc'teryx

Prêt-à-porter beachside
Whisk yourself away to Cheval
Blanc St-Barth Isle de France, on
luscious St Bart's in the French
Caribbean. Here, models give
wares from the glitzy resort's
boutique a twirl in a daily fashion
show on the beach. Expect that
little number by Pucci to get your
credit card in a sweat.

Cute as a button
You thought buttons were
for fastening clothes? Think
again. Sew some spare ones
that have four holes to a piece
of heavy fabric (don't sew
them too tightly – you need
space behind them), using
just two of the holes for the
thread. Slot the wires or posts
of a pair of earrings through
the free holes, and voilà, a
neat way to keep all your
earrings together ready for
storage in your jewellery roll.

Packing: wash 'n' go

Step away from that hotel laundry. Save your money by using these ideas for keeping clothes sparkling.

**Never mind a
room with a view…**

What about a room with a washer-dryer? This essential bit of kit is increasingly available in hotel rooms, including:

- New Zealand: Heritage Hotels (www.heritagehotels.co.nz).
- Europe: Citadines (www. citadines.com), which is also building a strong presence in Asia-Pacific.
- North America: check out Marriott (www.marriott.com),

Hilton (www.hilton.com) and Carlson Rezidor (www. carlsonrezidor.com) for their brands of extended-stay hotels, the type of accommodation in the USA and Canada that will lay on a washer-dryer, either in your room or in an on-site laundrette.

- Rest of the world: In destinations such as sub-Saharan Africa, India and South America, it's cheap as chips to send your clothes out for a service wash. Just don't expect your clothes to come back the same colour or shape…

My beautiful laundrette

Turn washday into sightseeing at these cool laundrettes:

RockOn Cleanicum Store
Brüsseler Str 74–76, Cologne, Germany (rockon.de/cleanicum)
Wash your clothes while buying some more at this fashion emporium for guys and gals. Hate shopping? Put your feet up and enjoy a fresh cup of java instead.

Laundromat Cafe
Various locations in Denmark and

Iceland and coming soon to Japan (thelaundromatcafe.com)
You won't be short of snacks or brain-food in these cafes lined with books and adorned with maps so you can plot your next travels.

BrainWash
1122 Folsom St, San Francisco, USA (brainwash.com)
You can laugh your socks off at the stand-up comedians while refreshing the contents of your suitcase here (and grab a burrito).

Machine Laundry Cafe
12 Salamanca Sq, Hobart, Tasmania Scrambled egg roti wrap is among the superior breakfast choices served up amid the soap suds at this buzzing cafe-laundrette.

The manual washing machine
Invest in a large water-tight aLOKSAK (loksak.com). Fill it with clothes, water and some liquid soap, knead, leave to soak for 10 minutes, then rinse. Simple.

Quick change
Need to clean an item of clothing overnight? After hand-washing, spread out the garment on a bath towel, roll it up tightly and wring (walk on the roll for extra oomph). If there's no radiator, hang the clean clothing close to the air-con. Finish off damp waistbands with the hairdryer.

Suds' laws
- Forget travel wash: what do you think the hotel soap is for? If you must pack detergent, choose soap-powder cakes over liquid sachets to protect against spills.
- Low-budget travellers should invest in a universal sink plug – or use a rolled-up sock.
- A long bungee cord will keep your suitcase shut and provide a strong washing line.

Packing: plane travel

If there's one bag that needs careful packing, it's the one you'll take on board your flight.

Carry-on bag

Carry a capacious bag that can be instantly opened for easy delving; you don't want to be constantly zipping and unzipping. A structured rather than a soft bag is preferable, to stop your possessions spilling everywhere when you put it down.

Remember to close your bag on leaving the plane – if it hasn't got a zip or clasp, tuck a shawl or cardigan tightly over the top and plonk a cheap, heavy item such as a book on top.

Contents

Keep order within your bag by compartmentalising items such as keys, money and documents, leaving big items such as books and tablets loose. Invest in a multi-pocket inner specially designed for the job (often sold in the in-flight shop), which can also be transferred across your bags, or specialist pods sold at Muji, Ikea and the like. Plastic folders with a press-stud close are good for keeping documents neat and safe. Go retro with a pencil case.

If you can't take the heat...
Boy-band star James McElvar thought he'd found a canny way to avoid the excess luggage charge: he put on six T-shirts, four jumpers, three pairs of jeans, two pairs of joggers, two jackets and two hats before boarding. But he soon regretted not splashing the cash. On landing he was whisked to hospital to be treated for heat exhaustion.

An inexpensive alternative is to use old make-up bags or even basic plastic ones: opt for the transparent Ziploc sort meant for the freezer so that you can see what you're looking for. Travelling with the family? Always take a plastic bag to use as a bin.

Don't rely on airline freebies: take your own survival kit. A comfy journey should be guaranteed if you've packed an eye mask, earplugs, lip balm, moisturiser, dental floss, tissues, painkillers, toothbrush and toothpaste.

A pair of socks is useful if wearing sandals or flip-flops.

Clothes

Keep warm or cool by dressing in layers. You'll be thankful for a cardigan/shawl if they whack up the air-con.

There's a reason why some airlines provide special pyjama sets to their premium customers in business and first class. Loose, comfortable clothing is the only way to dress when you're racing through the skies in a confined space. A lightweight change of clothes, with no cinches, works well (and will be a blessing if your luggage goes astray).

If you're travelling long-haul, pack a pair of 'toilet socks' that can be chucked in the laundry bag/wash at your destination. You won't want to keep pulling shoes on those puffy tootsies every time you head for the bathroom.

Dry run
Really want to be light on your feet? Substitute heavy liquids for multi-purpose solids.

• Choose a soap bar or dry shampoo, rather than liquids. There are all-in-one soap bars that work for teeth, clothes, body and hair. Dr Bronner's solid castile soap has a tea-tree scent and anti-microbial properties.

• Use dry face wipes that reanimate in water (rather than the heavy moist ones or make-up remover). Deodorants, perfumes and most cosmetics now come in solid sticks.

• For a truly obsessive level of liquid-to-solid packing, try dry toothpaste or make some yourself: squeeze out enough dots of toothpaste for each day of your trip, coat in a small amount of baking powder, then leave to dry. When you need them, just chew and brush. The spare-button bags supplied with new clothing (take out the buttons!) are a good place in which to store these.

- How to pack for any trip -

Packing: tech tips

Get the most from your technology – harness its power to help you pack less.

Ditch the newspaper and potboiler – that's what e-readers are for. All your reading matter can be kept in a slim electronic volume, accessible at the touch of a finger. These gadgets are often better for reading than tablets because their battery life is longer and the screens are specially adapted.

A lot of electrical products share the same style of charger these days. However, if you need a number of different ones, avoid a tangled heap of cables by investing in a multi-charger.

Many of us are happy enough to use our mobile or tablet as a camera, but for others a compact,

Stay in charge
Remember to charge before you go – there's nothing worse than a drained battery when you're miles from an electric socket. In addition, it's a legal requirement in the USA that your mobile device be charged when boarding a flight.

bridge or even SLR camera might be essential. If high-quality photos are a must but space is at a premium, good compact-system cameras take SLR-quality photos but aren't as bulky. Wi-fi-enabled cameras make downloading and sharing photos on social media really easy.

Don't forget, your smartphone is likely to have a torch, compass and alarm clock built in, but be aware that some of these functions may require data-use, so check how this will be reflected in your bill.

Working on the go? A laptop isn't vital if you own a tablet because these can be Bluetoothed to keyboards. In fact, some keyboards even serve as a protective screen cover.

Set your music free and party on the road with a Bluetooth speaker. Mini versions can weigh less than 250g and still pack a punch. Remember, if you stream tunes on the go you might be charged for data usage. An MP3 player might still be the better option.

Pool that power
If you're travelling with friends, consider pooling tech; there's little point in everyone taking the same gear.

Stayin' alive
Modern lithium batteries shouldn't be run down completely – keep them charged between 40 and 80 per cent to extend their life.

Packing: teach the kids

Plenty of time and patience, that's what you'll need to teach your kids to pack.
Keep calm and give it a go (counting to 10 under your breath can help).

Whip up excitement by starting the packing process early. This way you can also soothe any fears by discussing what you'll be doing and, therefore, what you'll need to take. Letting little ones buy something new for the trip – a toy, book or game, even an item of clothing, not to be used before departure – will maintain a sense of anticipation.

Ask younger children to draw their packing list, turning a chore into a fun game from the start. Make sure they draw a little box to tick off each item once it's packed, to keep them involved. Even numbers can be brought into play, depending on their age, working out how many of each item is needed for the holiday.

Get your children to lay out their clothes and possessions in piles for the different days you'll be away. This will help introduce them to the logic of only packing a certain amount of each item. Review these piles together. In this way, you can double-check exactly what will be packed and gently help them gather anything they've missed.

But don't just steam in and override their choices, otherwise they'll be put off helping in the future. Diplomacy is the best way to change that pink elephant for a toothbrush.

How many toys?

More is best when packing for children, says William Gray, editor of 101 familyholidays.co.uk: 'You want to avoid your child packing their whole soft-toy collection, yet I have fond memories of our two children "nesting" on every flight they took from the age two to 12. They'd arrange a dozen cuddly toys each around themselves, on the fold-out trays, stuck to the Velcro headrest covers etc. If they can fit the toys in their hand luggage, I don't see a problem with this. If they're happy and relaxed, so are their parents. Just remember to check for missing teddies before disembarking.

'Avoid teenagers resorting to their smartphones by encouraging them to get into a really good series of books a few days *before* you travel so that they'll be sure to pack them. But don't get too confrontational over phone/tablet use with teens on holiday. It inevitably leads to a row or big sulk. Far better to pack the holiday with loads of exciting activities, so that they don't miss their devices.'

App happy

Download travel-themed apps to keep kids busy. **A Parcel of Courage**, for pre-schoolers, is an illustrated storybook in which kids help grandma overcome her fear of flying. **Barefoot World Atlas**, for 9-11 year-olds, inspires young explorers. Youngsters can share stories and pictures of their travels on **Scribble Press**. The app features more than 300 stamps, stickers and more to let little imaginations fly.

Packing: quiz

What type of traveller are you – budget, eco-conscious, luxury, adventurer? Try our quiz to discover your true wandering spirit.

1. You never travel without…

a) The emergency number for your travel insurance company.
b) A bar of biodegradable soap.
c) Your penknife.
d) A pashmina.

2. Embarking on a 24hr plane journey, what's your mindset?

a) You're trying to remember how to get an upgrade.
b) You're working out how you are going to offset all that carbon.
c) You're totting up how many countries you could visit if you made the return journey overland.
d) You're wondering whether they serve Cristal or Krug in first class.

3. Given the choice, your preferred accommodation would be…

a) A hotel room with its own bathroom.
b) A yurt.
c) A bivvy bag.
d) The presidential suite.

4. The only way to travel around is by…

a) Squeezing into an economy hire car.
b) Using your own two feet.
c) Kayak.
d) Private jet, of course.

**5. You keep in touch
with home by…**
a) Sending a postcard.
b) Updating your blog, when you
can find an internet cafe.
c) You might give them a ring when
you get down off that mountain.
d) Darling, who turns off roaming?

**6. You've always
wanted to see…**
a) The Eiffel Tower.
b) Loggerhead turtles.
c) The South Pole.
d) The inside of the Royal Suite at
Dubai's Burj Al Arab.

7. You'd never be seen on the beach without…
a) A windbreak.
b) A bag for your rubbish.
c) Socks and sandals.
d) A pair of Rick Aviators by Tom Ford.

8. The perfect way to relax on holiday is to…
a) Lie on a sunbed with a good book.
b) Salute the sun.
c) Paraglide.
d) Indulge in a four-hand massage in the spa.

9. It's dinnertime, what's your preferred place to eat?
a) A restaurant favoured by the locals.
b) Somewhere that has vegan dishes on the menu.
c) A campfire.
d) The nearest three Michelin-starred joint.

10. For your next trip, you're thinking of visiting…
a) Athens and staying in an Air BnB.
b) A great little yoga retreat in France you've heard about.
c) Everest Base Camp.
d) The Caribbean, island-hopping by yacht.

Mainly As: You're a budget traveller. You may be operating on a tight budget, but you know how to make the most of it and have fun, too.

Mainly Bs: You're an eco-conscious traveller. The world is your oyster, but you're determined to protect it along the way.

Mainly Cs: You're an adventurer. Who said it's better to travel than to arrive, was that you?

Mainly Ds: You're a luxury traveller. Money is no object so why not spend it around the globe?

Packing: courier services
Hate the idea of packing light? Then get someone else to carry your luggage.

Sending your luggage ahead sounds like something a serious toff would have done when embarking on a Grand Tour in the 1700s. Yet it seems we're going back to the future in the 21st century, as reflected by the increasing demand for luggage courier services.

In fact, a whole industry has emerged around porterage for travellers prepared to pay the price for having their bags delivered from door to door. Not that those prices are always as steep as you

Safety first
- **Always label your luggage. Pack a second label inside with your contact details.**
- **Share friends' clothing between bags in case anyone's luggage goes missing.**
- **Never pack precious items in hold luggage.**
- **Lock your bag to ensure your insurance is valid. Travelling to the USA? Your locks must be TSA-approved (tsa.gov).**

might think; many companies compare favourably with the charges demanded by airlines to put luggage in the hold.

It's a very attractive concept. No heavy case to drag around, no bag-drop queue to endure. You simply arrive in your resort to find your luggage in your room, waiting to be unpacked – and many five-star resorts will even take care of that, too.

Courier companies pride themselves on the security of their transfers and tracking systems allow customers to chart the progress of their luggage throughout its journey. Money-back guarantees for late delivery are standard.

For more details, check out these courier services, which operate worldwide:
- **First Luggage** (*firstluggage.com*)
- **Send My Bag** (*sendmybag.com*)
- **Extra Baggage** (*extra-baggage.com*).

Bag in Japan?
The Japanese have long seen the sense in getting someone else to shoulder their bag burden, and courier services are standard in hotels and railway stations alongside plenty of companies that offer door-to-door delivery. Most Japanese tour-operators also offer this as part of a package. Costs are minimal, around US$12–24 per bag.

Method: rolling

Join the jet set. Regular travellers swear by the rolling method for its space-saving, crease-free advantages.

For coats, jackets, T-shirts, jumpers, shirts, blouses, dresses
Step 1: Hold up the garment with the front facing you, then pinch the shoulders halfway along between your thumb and forefinger, bringing your other fingers to the front. If the garment has a hood, flip it back.

Step 2: Twist your wrists inwards to turn the sleeves to the back, bringing the outer edges of the sleeves to touch each other.

Step 3: For ease, lay the garment on a flat surface, front down, with the neck/waistband towards you. Flatten out the sleeves. Bring the neck down to the base of the garment.

Step 4: Tuck your fingers in the fold of the sleeves and tidy the garment into a neat rectangle.

Step 5: Tightly roll up the garment. Next!

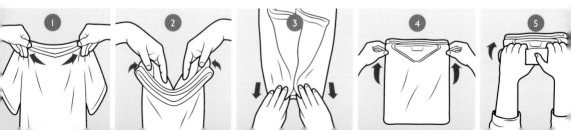

For trousers, shorts, tube dresses, straight skirts
Step 1: Hold up the item with the front facing you.

Step 2: Fold the garment in half vertically – follow the tailoring. Trousers, for example, can fold at the crotch or along the centre crease of the leg.

Step 3: Tightly roll up the garment to the hem.

Variation: Alternatively, don't fold the garment in half, just tightly roll it from the collar/waistband to its hem.

👍 **Saves space, avoids creases.**

👎 **Technique needs mastering for speed. Must fully unpack at destination.**

⭐ **Best for: trolley cases, large suitcases, holdalls, backpacks.**

– How to be a packing maestro –

Packing rolled clothing
Step 1: Pack the rolled items tightly, side by side, to cover the bottom of your bag or case.

Step 2: Create layers depending on the depth of your luggage.

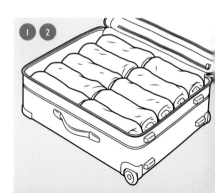

Method: folding

Probably the most popular way to pack, yet the folding method is criticised for
an origami-style approach that keeps the travel-iron manufacturers in business.

For coats, jackets, T-shirts, jumpers, shirts, blouses, dresses
Step 1: Hold up the garment with the front facing you, then pinch the shoulders between your thumb and forefinger, with your other fingers at the front. If the garment has a hood, flip it back.

Step 2: Twist your wrists inwards to turn the sleeves to the back, bringing the outer edges of the sleeves to touch each other.

Step 3: Lay the garment on a flat surface, front down, with the neck towards you. Flatten out the sleeves. Fold the neck to the base.

Step 4: Tuck your fingers in the fold of the sleeves and tug, tidying the garment into a neat rectangle.

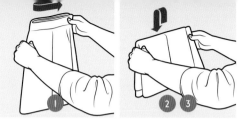

Packing folded clothing
Step 1: Stack folded items, like you would in a chest of drawers, to the full depth of your bag or case.

For trousers, shorts, tube dresses, straight skirts
Step 1: Fold the garment in half vertically – follow the tailoring. Trousers, for example, can fold at the crotch or along the centre crease of the leg.

Step 2: Fold in half again.

Step 3: Continue to fold until the desired size is achieved.

👍 **Mobile chest of drawers** – no need to fully unpack at destination.

👎 **Creases.** Less space-saving than rolling.

⭐ **Best for:** trolley cases, large suitcases, holdalls, backpacks.

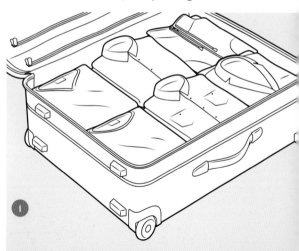

Method: bundling

As seen on YouTube. You may feel you've better things to do with your time than perfect such wizardry.

Step 1: Lay a jacket flat on a table with its collar down and arms out.

Step 2: Lay a long-sleeved shirt on the jacket at 180 degrees, collar up, arms out. Position the top of the shirt collar about halfway down the jacket, leaving a space between both garments' collars. This is where you'll later create a core around which the bundle will fold.

Step 3: Layer your next garment in the direction of the jacket and the following one in the direction of the original shirt, then continue alternating in this way.

Step 4: Fold trousers in half vertically and add them on the horizontal (shorts, too). Line up the waistband with the seam of the arm, and, like the other garments, alternate left and right.

Step 5: Continue to build the bundle so that it progresses from most-tailored clothes to least-tailored ones, with T-shirts being the last to join the heap.

Step 6: Put underwear between the collars to create the core. Wrap the first T-shirt around the items, sleeves first, body second. Continue to wrap T-shirts around the core, one by one, in this way. Coil trousers/shorts around the core, followed by more sleeves then body areas for the shirts and jacket, smoothing out fabric as you go until you have one big bundle.

👍 **Fewer creases than folding.**

👎 **Some items will be inaccessible until you fully unpack. Requires you to be strategic about space for other items, such as a toiletry bag.**

⭐ **Best for: trolley cases, large suitcases.**

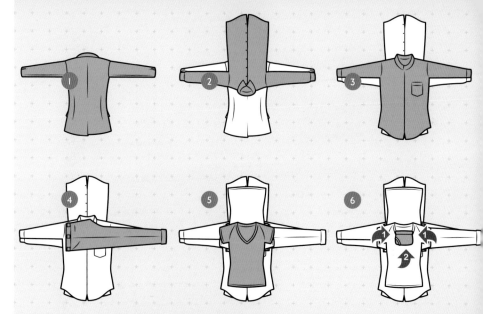

Method: stuffing

If you're the kind of traveller who likes to leave everything to the last minute, stuffing is for you. Chaos rather than method is invoked. Fast, furious – and possibly the worst way to pack.

Step 1: This method occupies a place beyond rules. Anything goes.

👍 **Works for all types of bag. You don't need to engage brain (can be done with a hangover/jet lag)**

👎 **Creases. Bad use of space. Guaranteed inaccessibility. Potential time wasted sitting on bag to get it to shut.**

★ **Best for: trolley cases, large suitcases, holdalls, backpacks.**

Steamy iron
If, on arrival, you open your case and find your favourite dress has more wrinkles than a Shar-Pei, hang it in a steamy bathroom. But don't assume those creases will just drop out – when the clothing becomes damp, you'll need to give it a couple of sharp shakes and pull it into shape.

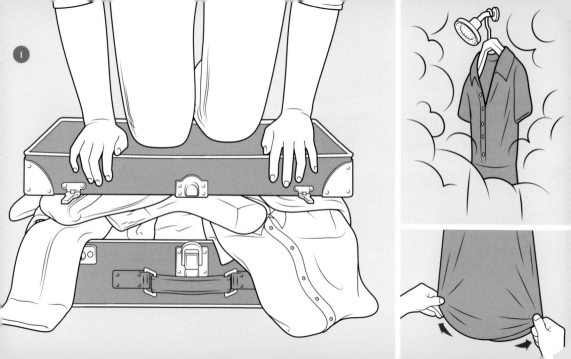

Method: layering tissue paper and scented bags
Favoured by fusspots and bridezillas.

Step 1: Follow the folding method, putting sheets of tissue between each layer. The truly pernickety can even fold tissue into each garment. Tuck silk pouches of lavender/cedarwood in gaps in your case or bag. Of course, it helps if you can enlist your staff to do this tiresome yet crucial task for you.

👍 No creases. Heady fragrances.

👎 Anyone watching you pack/unpack might think you have control issues.

⭐ Best for: trolley cases, large suitcases, holdalls.

Tactics
Don't pack ad hoc. Lay out everything you think you need and hone a packing strategy from there.

Method: creating compartments
The Russian-doll approach to packing is great for the (over-)organised traveller.

Buy pods and bags that allow you to pack items separately at stores such as Muji and Ikea, or choose lightweight expandable packing cubes, which are available from good department stores.

Beware, however, of choosing identical containers: consider colour coordination for quick identification of items. Look out for bespoke packing solutions, too, such as bra cases, jewellery rolls and shoe bags – the felt ones clean your shoes' uppers as a bonus.

Alternatively, save money by creating your own compartments:

- A large make-up bag could hold your delicates.
- Resealable kitchen bags are useful for small items such as cables and plugs.
- A good old-fashioned plastic bag keeps shoes separate.
- Plastic film-roll canisters and old glasses cases are ideal for protecting jewellery and storing coins/foreign currency.

👍 **Easily accessible.**

👎 **Could be expensive. Space is wasted on the containers themselves and they potentially add weight.**

⭐ **Best for: trolley cases, large suitcases, holdalls.**

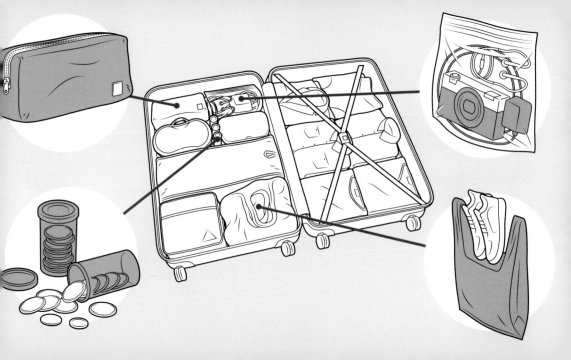

Method: filling gaps

Choose your preferred method – roll, fold or bundle. Stuff all gaps and edges in your luggage, and any recesses in packed items such as shoes, bra cups and hats. Socks, handkerchiefs, toiletry bags, plugs, jewellery cases, belts, ties, plus anything you don't mind being creased, are all good for filling these voids.

👍 Maximises space. Easily accessible.

👎 You'll need a good memory to remember after a long journey where you hid that vital item.

⭐ Best for: trolley cases, large suitcases, holdalls, backpacks.

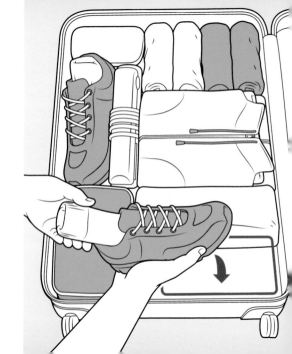

Method: bottom-heavy

However you pack, always keep heavy items such as shoes, toiletries, electronics and books at the bottom of your luggage. This gravity-friendly tactic will help reduce creases, too. But think accessibility – your coat may be heavy, but you should still pack it at the top, especially if headed to a destination where the weather is unreliable.

👍 Stops your case or bag falling on the person in front in the check-in queue – and won't be top-heavy when you're in motion. Helps reduce wrinkles.

👎 Backpackers may have accessibility issues.

⭐ Best for: trolley cases, large suitcases, holdalls, backpacks.

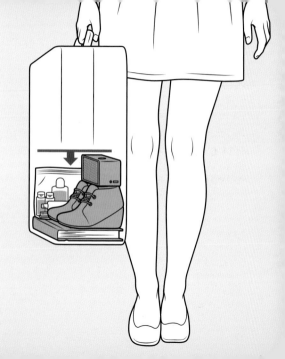

Method: keeping similar items together

Take organisation up a level by keeping similar clothes together. You'll be able to spot all T-shirts or dresses at a glance. And it's easy to check you're packing enough of each item too.

Size matters
Choose the size of your bag or case with care. Always fill it as near to capacity as possible to stop items moving around.

👍 **Instantly accessible choice of different styles of one item. Quick to unpack.**

👎 **Inefficient space-wise.**

⭐ **Best for:** trolley cases, large suitcases, holdalls, backpacks.

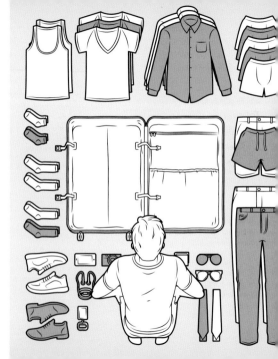

Method: keeping similar colours together

Take a tip from the fashionistas – ensure your favourite colours are well represented across your portable wardrobe.

Extra bag

Always pack a light, soft bag for packing those extra items you'll buy along the way. Or, if you manage to resist retail temptation, it'll be a handy sack for dirty clothes.

👍 You're good to go colour-coordinated.

👎 Style over substance – you'll squeeze less in your luggage.

⭐ Best for: trolley cases, large suitcases, holdalls, backpacks.

Method: Tetris-style

One for gamer geeks, this technique turns packing into a puzzle. Combine blocks of different shapes and sizes to form complete rows. Stack your rolled and/or folded clothes vertically or horizontally; there's no need to stick to one plane in this game. Beware, this method only really works if you can unpack fully at your destination – not recommended for backpackers on the move.

KonMari system

Japanese decluttering guru Marie Kondo suggests you stack vertically so you can see everything at a glance. But it requires a shallow case, like a drawer, because ideally you want just one layer. Use the system to micro-manage the contents using tailoring details. For example, fold several pairs of jeans in such a way that you can spot which is which by the stitching on the back pocket.

👍 Ultimate space-saver. Good for families – making a chore into a game.

👎 Need to be good at puzzles. The whole system is just one removal of an ill-placed item away from falling apart.

⭐ Best for: trolley cases, large suitcases.

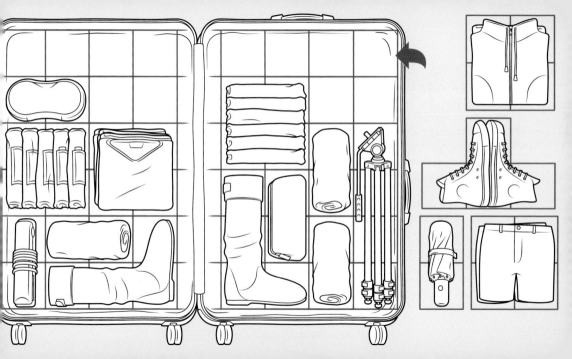

Method: backpack

The budget globetrotter's dilemma: how to organise the shove-it-all-in backpack.

Step 1: Keep the weight low and centred in the main body of the bag. For example, put shoes in the bottom (buy a pack with a self-contained bottom compartment, which is great for separating out soiled shoes and wet kit).

Step 2: Put liquids and toiletries in external side pockets.

Step 3: Watertight bags, such as aLOKSAKs, are useful for wet kit that must be taken in the main body of the bag.

Step 4: Roll, even stuff, but never fold – it's futile.

Step 5: Compression/vacuum sacks/expandable pods are great for minimising puffy items such as down jackets and sleeping bags. It can also be helpful to have similar items in easy-to-grab bags.

Step 6: Keep coats and essentials such as your wallet and phone at the top of your bag.

Step 7: Use carabiners to clip water bottle, travel pillow, roll mat and the like to the outside of your backpack.

Step 8: Put your backpack in its own waterproof cover – or pack the innards of your bag in plastic bags for waterproofing.

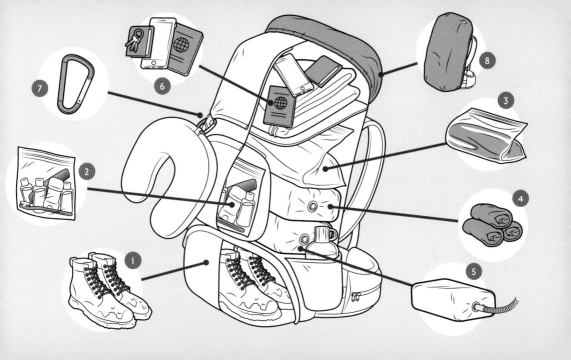

How to pack for **your** trip

Where are you going? City
The cool culture city

This kind of destination, while perhaps not so culturally unfamiliar, still demands careful suitcase strategy. From boho bars to cutting-edge galleries, the outfits and accessories you choose can seriously enhance your travel experience.

Many of the essentials will be digital. Want to hotfoot it across town to bag that gold-dust restaurant reservation/show ticket/cheap hotel room? Then download interactive offline maps or apps that access wi-fi without resorting to roaming charges.

And while the scene may be hot, the weather might not. Layers are key for looks that balance comfort and style.

Packing essentials

- Comfortable shoes: we're not talking ugly-yet-commodious; your kicks should be stylish enough to both dangle from a bar stool in a hipster cafe and sit happily on your feet while pounding miles of pavement

- Sunglasses: true, it might not always be sunny, but life in the city, from the glare of the morning-after to that dazzling check-in moment at the hotel (off the red-eye flight), demands sleek shades.

- Cashmere jumper: this softie packs down to almost nothing and is the perfect defence against ferocious summer air-con in hotels and on the plane. It is also a lightweight, smart-looking, shiver-saving layer if the weather really turns chilly.

Travelling to America?
Pack photo ID. You may be over 21, but in many states you'll be 'carded' if a barman thinks you're under 35. NOTE: taking your passport bar-hopping isn't smart.

Case study: Stockholm
Winter's brutal temperatures and the design-conscious addresses of SoFo enforce the need for a winter jacket that's both sharp-cut and seriously insulated.

In summer, don't go anywhere without swims (from local label Eytys, obviously). From the beaches of Rålambshov Park to the leafy shores of Kungsholmen there's always the chance to make a splash.

Love your denim? This is the country of brands such as Nudie Jeans. Save space in your case and shop at the source.

Where are you going? City
The exotic city

It may be hot, but leaving bare skin to steam may not be appropriate. Natural fibres are your friend here. A cotton shirt will preserve modesty, ensure entrance into temples and keep the sun from sizzling shoulders. Shorts should not be 'short'; deep, secure pockets are a plus. Meanwhile, you want your feet to both breathe and sit pretty, should a smart rooftop restaurant appear on the agenda: ditch the flip-flops in favour of decent walking sandals.

Packing essentials

- Swims: it matters not if you're miles from the coast, from urban beaches to hotels and even hostels with a pool, there's usually a chance to cool down with a swim…. Or a trip to the local water park.
- Rohan-style travel trousers: lightweight, quick-drying and, these days, not nearly so fugly. Choose ones that zip off to make shorts for dual function.
- Daypack: this needs to be secure, lightweight and, ideally, made out of soft, natural, breathable fibre that doesn't induce chafing or sweating when carried against bare skin.

Going to Singapore? Don't pack your packets. There's a tax on bringing cigarettes into the country, even for personal use, while vaporisers aren't allowed in at all. Although it's not illegal to buy cigarettes, it is an offence to smoke in most public places.

Case study: Delhi

Pack an open mind; there's nowhere quite like Delhi to bring on a white-hot case of culture shock. The motto of most travellers to India's urban centres is 'be prepared for anything', and this extends to packing.

For most, the Indian lifestyle is truly foreign and can be life-changing. Those not usually given to sketching or diary keeping might find themselves moved to create. Pack a notepad.

Head coverings are a must at many sights; a sarong serves well and has multiple other functions, including shielding your face from city smog. And scrap those tatty ethnic trousers. In this increasingly middle-class city you won't be welcome looking like a '60s hippie.

Where are you going? Wilderness
Wild and windy

No matter which end of the world you tour the wilds, the same packing principles remain. The elements will be both a marvel and a maverick force. Often finding yourself miles from shelter and civilisation, you'll need to carry protective kit.

Rough mountain tracks or wet grassy plains? Let the type of terrain dictate footwear. Advances in the design of walking shoes mean clunky hiking boots might not be essential, but a quick-drying, wind- and rain-proof shell or jacket will be. Large plastic bin liners, Ziploc® bags in different sizes and/or waterproof bag liners will keep kit dry when that squall comes in across the valley.

Packing essentials
Temperatures will vary wildly with weather, season and altitude, so embrace the layering system.
- Base layer: a high-wicking, close-fitting top and possibly bottoms. Merino wool is warmest and needs less frequent washing.
- Mid-layer: fleece or similar on top; quick-drying walking trousers on the bottom.
- Outer layer: a breathable waterproof/windproof jacket and trousers.
- Extra-warm layer: a down jacket for use at night can be spirit-lifting, and adds comfort on chilly damp days. Supplement with gloves, hat, scarf/buff for extra easily removable protection.

Crystal waters?
Pack some means of water purification – that stream water may look good enough to sup, but it might harbour parasites. A Web-tex survival straw is a neat bit of kit.

Case study: Scottish Highlands
There's a reason Scotland's wilderness stars in movies. With snow-blown glens, misty moors and lochs, no other UK landscape is as menacing. This isn't just aesthetics.

Pack a compass. If the weather closes in and phone/GPS signals drop out, you may need to take bearings. Go for one with a baseplate for easier reading and master the art before you head out. Insect repellent is essential for staying sane in summer; keep to higher ground to better avoid the notorious midges.

© Matt Munro

Where are you going? Wilderness
Hot and dry

 Retreat from the modern world into a land of big starry skies and wild, nature-dominated panoramas. From the alien salt flats of Bolivia's Salar de Uyuni and the dusty outback of the Brazilian Sertão to the dense, pristine forests north-west Tasmania, wilderness often comes at the price of connectivity… and electricity.

Pack expedition-style for self-sufficiency. A solar charger is essential for keeping GPS and phone topped up; and while you might be used to using the latter's torch, consider something more robust for this trip.

Packing essentials

- Cotton shirt: in warmer climes, you might want to substitute that hi-tech base layer for a lightweight, 100% cotton shirt. These are more versatile, working for both evening and daywear. Avoid those treated with water-repellent chemicals so that you benefit from cotton's natural wicking properties.

- Foldable drinking bottle: these save on space, but is that wilderness water drinkable? (See page 87.)
- First-aid kit: essential in parts of the world blissfully free of Walmart – or even a village shop. These are sold pre-packed but are best tailored to suit your needs and destination. Bare minimum: plasters (band-aids), bandages and cotton wool, painkillers/stomach upset pills, antiseptic cream, rehydration salts.

Wait a cotton-picking moment!

If you're out in warm, dry grasslands – such as those in the American South, sub-Saharan Africa and the Eurasian Steppe – bear in mind that crickets eat cotton. They have a special appetite for items with high thread counts, so keep those fine cotton towels and pricey linen shirts well hidden.

Case study: Arizona

Home to the Grand Canyon and the saguaro cactus-spiked Sonoran desert, Arizona is know for its fierce sun, even in winter, so cover your head, cowboy. But those canyons are cold at night, so fleece up. Horse riding is often the best way to explore, so wear comfortable trousers that will withstand thorny brush and long periods in the saddle.

© Mark Read

Where are you going? Afloat
Europe

 For independent-spirited 'sailors', Europe has much to offer – from Greece's vast ferry network to the canal boats of France and Britain's old industrial waterways, Scandinavia's efficient passenger ships to the posh yachts plying the pristine waters off Croatia's rugged coast.

Cruise ships these are not, but they are often surprisingly well kitted out, equipped with cabins, bedding and shower rooms. However, space will always be an issue. For ease of boarding, and stowing bags, it's crucial to consider luggage size and style. Wheelie bags can be cumbersome on cobbled, uneven dock terrain. Duffle bags with zip-out backpack straps are the best buy: portable, easily stuffed under seats and in the corners of cabins, and a good seat/cushion substitute.

Packing essentials

- Waterproof shoes: some landings will be wet, and while flip-flops might just about cut it, are you sure you can keep them on while scrambling down a jetty carrying your luggage?
- Waterproof/windproof jacket: you won't be able to resist those starry skies up on deck, but even in summer it can be brisk and breezy out there. Prolong the pleasure with a lightweight outer layer that can withstand wind and sudden squalls.
- A fistful of dollars: or, rather, euros. On some of Europe's smaller islands, ATMs are still a rarity. Carry sufficient local currency to get by.

Prickly issue
In Croatia, be wary of bays and beaches where sea urchins cling to rocks. These spiky black creatures can seriously maim if stood upon. Almost every Croatian coastal resort/village sells rubbery water-shoes, which are cheap and invaluable when swimming, rock-hopping and mooring your boat.

Case study: Greek islands
The rule of thumb when packing for this part of the world is 'half the kit, double the money'. A burdensome bag will really reduce the joys of this liberating experience.

A packing must? A light, windproof jacket for overnight crossings and to protect against the *meltemi*, the notorious wind that batters the Greek islands in summer.

Where are you going? Afloat
In the tropics

 Whether you're sailing the South Pacific, cruising the Caribbean or exploring the Galapagos Islands aboard a luxury expedition ship, you've spent some serious money getting to your destination, so don't stint on packing. Many cruise ships have dress codes, so travelling light should not be your main preoccupation. Once in your cabin, that bag can be unpacked and forgotten.

That said, you don't need to be trailing a retinue of steamer trunks with enough outfits to clothe a small island nation. Look smart but think strategic by using our packing tips below.

Packing essentials

• Dress for dinner: as the demographic of cruise passengers has become more diverse, so has attire. Few issues create more confusion than what you're supposed to wear in the dining room, and most ships still have a dress code. Check out the Cruise Critic website (cruisecritic.co.uk), which offers an overview of the different requirements.

• Lightweight shirt: going too casual at many ports of call or even by the pool is often a no-no. Swimwear and vest tops can be made smarter when overlaid with a well-pressed cotton shirt. It's good for sun protection, too.

• Shoes: don't fill your case with footwear. Instead, pick two or three pairs that can serve multiple purposes, and colour-coordinate formalwear to match one pair of dressy shoes.

Don't go commando

Ditch the camouflage shorts in Grenada and Jamaica: in these and other parts of the Caribbean, wearing camouflage print is outlawed.

Case study: Caribbean cruise

Love to take in a dip in every port? Pack your own mask and snorkel to avoid wasting time in the scrum for kit.

Most cabins provide soap and shampoo, if not body lotion and conditioner, but if you're picky, pack your own.

Over-the-door shoe/toiletry bags can help to maximise storage in cabin quarters.

The price of water/soda on board is often very inflated. Some cruise lines let you bring your own, so pack a daypack for when shopping for refills (and for souvenirs).

© doodah_stock/Getty Images, ©Monica and Michael Sweet/Getty Images

Where are you going? Beach
The blustery, rugged beach

 If you want more than bronzing from the beach, pack your walking boots and go coastal to spots where simple sun-seekers are rarely seduced. When it comes to packing, think action. Trekking boots or fishing tackle? Save on space, and possibly money, too, by phoning ahead to see what can be hired at your destination. Will it be riding Wales' surf or tackling the long-distance walking trails that carve up the limestone karst landscapes of Croatia's mountain-backed coast? Saddling up for a hack around Denmark's broad, sand beaches or biking New Zealand's glacier-hewn bays? Whatever rocks your boat, plan ahead.

Packing essentials
- Wetsuit: kids go in whatever the weather, but if you want more than a quick dip, consider a half-suit. Not a huge investment, but these buy you more swim time in chilly waters and have become de rigueur in British waters.
- Waterproof shoes: waterproof walking boots or rubber shoes are best. When repacking, wrap each in a plastic bag and stuff with dirty linen to save space.
- Talcum powder: when it comes to ridding skin of sticky, damp sand, there's nothing as effective as talc – just sprinkle, rub and remove, then slip socks back on to hike onwards in comfort. Talc also doubles as dry shampoo, stops backpacks chafing shoulders and, should there be a heatwave, cools clammy sheets.

Exploring Scandinavia's shores? On the region's seafood safaris, fishers offer insight (and lunch) on lobster-farming, netting mussels, shucking oysters and more. Warm hats recommended!

Case study: Cornwall
Contrary to British belief, you cannot bring on warm weather by dressing for it. Cornwall's golden sands and its much-vaunted microclimate may bode well but, even in summer, it pays to come prepared.

Think sweaters, along with hopeful swimsuits and a lightweight anorak. Drysacks are brilliant for keeping grit and moisture from terrorising your tech. And consider packing a windbreak. Protection on elemental beaches can be the difference between fun and fail.

© Matt Munro

Where are you going? Beach
The barefoot, exotic beach

 When hitting the sand, you need little more than a colourful swimsuit and a smile, right? That's the spirit on a tropical beach break. But from the islands of Thailand to the white-sand atolls of the Maldives and the sun- and fun-sure beaches of Brazil, there are some key packing requirements. For example, coral often comes with both mesmerising colours and a sting. A basic medical kit may seem a bit Boy Scout, but it's essential, especially if you're cast away on a far-flung island. Oh, and that swimsuit? Take extras. Humidity means things don't dry well and swimming togs are likely to be your daily outfit.

Packing essentials

- Aloe vera: with great medicinal and cooling qualities, lotions made from the plant's juice make the best after-sun solution. If it grows locally, simply strip the outer leaves and slather the inner goo on to skin.
- Nature-friendly sunscreen: the world's coral is getting a bashing from overfishing, El Niño and rising ocean temperatures, so don't add to its problems by layering on the sunscreen before swimming. Cover up with a T-shirt or pack creams that eschew harmful oxybenzone.
- Wet wipes: you may not be a middle-aged mum, but these are great for coping in skeezy loos, freshening up in lieu of a shower, cooling hot face and hands, sanitising cuts and scratches, and even sprucing up dusty sandals.

Patch it up

Even practised beach bunnies burn in these climes. Try the new 'smart' skin patches, which track the skin's exposure to harmful UV rays.

Case study: Thailand

In other parts of the world it may not be considered manly, but in Thailand both men and women can celebrate the sarong and a locally-bought cotton one is both a norm and a necessity. It's a useful shield against both freezing bus air-conditioning and fierce sun, and also doubles as a beach blanket, sheet and bath towel (with a quick rinse in between).

Duct tape is also your friend. You may have a mosquito net over your bed, but chances there'll be a hole (or five). Also useful for patching ripped backpacks… and taping that increasingly annoying travel companion's mouth shut. Jokes aside (we hope), tape is a handy fix. But pack your own net if you're going Alex Garland-style remote where mozzie protection can't be guaranteed.

© Catherine Sutherland

Where are you going? Mountains
High-altitude/hard-to-access mountains

 The right footwear is paramount. Walking shoes are almost certainly not going to cut it; in this rugged terrain you'll need extra ankle support. But do you really need those pricey three-season hike boots? It depends how far you're going and in what weather. Whatever you choose, never head off into the wilds without your boots being worn in. You don't want to be battling with blisters, miles from civilisation.

Packing essentials

- Proper socks: there's no point spending money on good shoes and then not choosing the right socks. Consider how you'll be exploring the wilderness – on foot, by bike, on horseback – and sock up accordingly. No matter where you are in the world, keeping feet insulated and dry can make a huge difference to your trip.
- Protective creams: there is nowhere, apart from sailing on the equator, that so demands high-factor suncream and lip balm, even on cool days. And don't forget extra-strength moisturisers: high equals dry, dehydrated skin.
- Medication: altitude sickness, which can occur from elevations of 2,500m, can be eased with local remedies such as coca tea (in the Andes), but it's always good to pack prescription Acetazolamide (Diamox) pills, because it's impossible to really know if, when or how hard acute mountain sickness might strike.

Medications
Carry a prescription if travelling with medication in the Caucasus, and declare the items on your customs' form. Check the legal local limits before you go.

Case study: Himalayas

The Himalayas are the crowning glory for mountain lovers. Everest may headline the gig, but the region's prayer-flag-strewn passes show that these mountains are most notable for their mosaic of cultures.

Dress respectfully. The Himalayas have sacred summits and peaks that are home to places of pilgrimage. Don't miss the chance to tour temples by lacking sufficient clothing (a locally bought sarong will do). Offerings will be gratefully received – small change in local currency or EFL text books.

© Marvin Suria-Ramos

Where are you going? Mountains
Lower-altitude/easy-to-access mountains

 Both wild and, in parts, well manicured, the lower-altitude or easier-access mountains offer trips to suit ascetics and aesthetes alike. These are the kinds of peaks – from Upstate New York to Italy's Apennines – where, since Victorian times, the great and good have come for restorative breaks in spa hotels and lakeside lodges.

The 'getting there' has always been part of the fun: arriving, as in Switzerland, on some of the world's first tourist-focused trains.

So packing needs to be stylish and strategic. Are your walking boots presentable enough to pass muster in a grand hotel lobby, should you want to pop in for that can't-miss cocktail? And will your designer backpack really survive that high mountain pass?

Packing essentials

- A gourmet appetite: forget frugal and filling mountain food. From the South Tyrol of Italy and Austria, to France, Switzerland and North America's east and west coast ranges, the mountains have become synonymous with good eating, the wild outpost for many a celebrity chef. Pack a credit card and dine in hotels and lodges with stupendous settings.
- Public transport timetables: from narrow-gauge railways to cable cars and lake ferries, transport in the mountains is a joy. It's utterly geared to getting travellers to the summit efficiently.
- Swimwear: with mountains come lakes. Or spa pools and hot tubs with a valley view.

Climbing Kilimanjaro?
You'll pass through five temperate climates in just a few days, so pack light layers for each season – but test first that you can wear them all and still move...

Case study: Switzerland
The Alps put on their prettiest shows in the 18th-century painters' peaks – Jungfrau, Matterhorn, Eiger. These summits, where mountain tourism was born, are for those with deep pockets and daring spirits.

Today, the Swiss mountains won't shun the jeans-and-sneakers brigade but pack a blazer/suit jacket to instantly dress up for smoother access into smart hotels.

These peaks are capricious; come the fog or a storm, they might become momentarily inaccessible – so pack a book.

© Matt Munro

Where are you going? Tropics/Jungle
Rainforest expeditions

 Packing for protection in the tropics is paramount. Your most likely modes of transport to explore this part of the world will be exposed: canoes, kayaks, jeeps and your own two feet. It's hot, but you'll need to cover up. You may be here to see the big mammals – the howler monkeys and jaguar of the Amazon or orangutans and tigers of Sumatra – but the most prevalent beasties are the smaller, biting kind. The other stinger is humidity, which will play havoc with everything from skin to suitcases if you're unprepared.

Packing essentials
- Shoulder the burden: a sturdy backpack is best for this terrain but a strong duffel bag works OK. Ditch the rolling suitcase; it will be wheelie useless on dirt trails and when hopping from canoes or jeeps.
- Quick-dry: the tropics can cool down at night so you'll need layers, but ensure they're made of quick-drying material (not cotton) or you'll be clammy and chilly. Layers also protect against determined bugs that will penetrate thin fabric to get a bite.
- Itchy and scratchy: insect repellent containing DEET (diethyltoluamide) and an anti-itch ointment are must-haves. It's also worth packing hydrocortisone cream to treat troublesome, swelling bites, or get some relief with a little gadget that calms maddening bites with a Piezoelectric charge.

Struggling to see anything?
Animals can't see the red colour spectrum, so at dusk or dawn, a head-torch with a red bulb setting will keep bugs at bay and help you to spot wildlife.

Case study: Amazon
Water, water everywhere... from rainfall to boggy riverbanks and dripping foliage, this part of the world is wet. It gives life to iridescent tree frogs and the Technicolor fungi that clings to trees like aliens. It also gets into everything you own and wear.

Waterproof hiking shoes are a must, topped off with waders to keep legs dry and protected. Dry bags and backpack rain-covers are great, but pack light. If possible, stow your main bag at your gateway destination and travel with a daypack.

Where are you going? Tropics/Jungle
Culture in the jungle

 The jungle hides many sightseeing secrets. From Cambodia's ancient kingdom of Angkor to Colombia's Ciudad Perdida, Java's sprawling temple of Borobudur to the Mayan pyramids of Mexico, it's worth battling through the humidity and undergrowth to get to these cultural treasures. Be aware, though, that this terrain is as tricky to pack for as a rainforest expedition, demanding much of the same kit but with the extra requirement that you dress for cultural sensitivity and pack to maximise cultural enrichment. Bulky books are out, but specialist digital guides can really help bring these historical sites to life.

Packing essentials

- A proper camera: yes, we know that smartphones do a decent job, but in low jungle light they won't see the intricate temple carvings for the trees. A flash and diffuser add a professional edge to this kind of photo, and only a few grams to luggage weight.
- Light sarong: once again, this fail-safe cover-up prevents the wearing of vest/tank tops from being tantamount to indecent exposure at religious sites.
- Light-headed: these sights can be soul-lifting, but the treks to them are often arduous. Pack light but bear in mind that the nights will be cooler, especially at higher altitudes. Keep wet/humid clothes and boots for daytime, and dry/warmer clothing in a plastic/dry bag for nightwear.

DEET warning
Bug repellent containing DEET corrodes some plastics and can leach the colour out of clothes/nail polish. It can also destroy your camera in a flash, so take care when applying.

Case study: Cambodia
The bustle of Phnom Penh and the boutique beach retreats increasingly attract travellers to Cambodia, but most come for one place: Angkor, the sprawling jungle-tangled ancient kingdom whose icon is the Angkor Wat temple complex.

Navigating sun-blasted paths and steep steps, plus biking the sandy trails, is hot work. Pack high-wicking shirts (with sleeves that can be rolled down) and long shorts to preserve your cool and your modesty. Chilly dawn trips require fleece and socks.

© Mark Read

Where are you going? Alpine
The chic snow scene

 If the season doesn't deliver champagne powder, you'll still be guaranteed premium fizz off-piste on this type of ski-and-be-seen trip. From the Windsor-endorsed inns of Klosters-Serneus in Switzerland to the mink stole-stuffed slopes of Courchevel, France, and the A-lister hub of Aspen, Colorado, to the old-money retreats of Zürs in Austria, you should pack to sparkle like snow under starlight. But do some research: does your resort attract the Russians and Ray-Bans set or is it more a Savile Row-inspired après scene? You might want to pack posh but not Posh (and Becks).

Packing essentials

- Skis and suits: in some of these high-flying resorts you'll be expected to dress for dinner. Jacket and tie will be as important as thermals and mitts.
- Retro *riche*: it changes with the alpine wind, but retro is currently the cool look to be wearing in the cold. Seek out labels such as M. Miller and Moncler for 1970s-style belted jackets in luxe fabrics, along with the much-coveted fur-lined Kask ski helmet.
- Accessorise at altitude: can't afford the full couture kit? Get signature accessories. Louis Vuitton fur scarf? Check. Nordic-inspired Gucci sweater? Check. The latest Swedish Yniq ski goggles? Check – and check you out.

Ski Japan
There's probably nowhere cooler to ski than Japan. But you'd better know how to deal with bottomless powder. Pack fat skis (or better still, a board) plus very warm socks.

Case study: Telluride
This boho Colorado mountain town has both the altitude and the attitude. It's where stars come for snowy R&R; where they can slip on their boots and blend in. Civvie skiers here are too cool to piste-stalk celebs.

Dress down, with street-cool skiwear; the look is more Spyder than Gucci snoods and Fendi shades. The off-piste scene is arty, so pack your knowledge of blues, bluegrass and micro-brews, along with your pre-booking for dinner at one of the gastro landmarks.

Where are you going? Alpine
The cheap snow scene

 Long before you even reach for the suitcase, ensure you research the latest snow report. Low cost also often means low altitude, so check the season's snow before booking and packing, as weather will dictate all.

It's never going to be truly cheap, but skiing can be cheerful... and pioneering. The savviest budget travellers select little-known but snow-sure resorts, such as Cauterets in the French Pyrénées, the 'sunny glade' of Poiana Brașov in Romania, and Vogel in Slovenia. But whether it's Zakopane in Poland or Bulgaria's Borovets, taking your own kit means you don't have to rely on woeful local ski-hire.

Packing essentials

- Get goggles: these are not something to rent in-resort. If they're available at all, they'll be pricey and you can buy a top-of-the-range pair for less at home. Go for ones with changeable lenses for sunshine and low light.
- Bargain bruises: if you're travelling on the cheap, it might be that you're testing the (frozen) waters as a first-time skier. In which case, bring a basic first-aid kit containing pills and potions for aching muscles, bruises and blisters. Buy in-resort and you'll discover that meds are big money.
- Snug slippers: after a day in boots, there's nothing like easing aching feet into comfy slippers. They're also invaluable on chilly floors and in shared chalets.

Albanian adventure

Cheap, with lots of powder, Albania is one for off-radar skiers. Bring your own kit, plus cash for a guide for exploring those 6,000ft summits.

Case study: Bosnia

When it comes to bargain snow breaks, Bosnia is the new Borovets (Eastern Europe's go-to cheap resort). Two decades on from the Yugoslav Wars, and following tough economic times, investment is going back into Balkan ski hubs. Resorts such as Jahorina are regaining the shine from when Sarajevo hosted the 1984 Winter Olympics.

Function, not fashion, equals fun here. If you have your own kit, take it: rental can be patchy. And if you're into off-piste, factor a guide into your budget. Mines are still a risk.

Where are you going? The Poles
Antarctic

 You're going outside… you may be some time. But, in fact, as most Antarctic trips are cruises, much of your southern exposure is likely to occur in the comfort of a very well-equipped ship, with short excursions by motorboat and on foot. As such, Antarctic forays don't require huge amounts of specialist gear, just a few carefully chosen items to keep you warm and dry. It's worth investing in a decent pair of insulated waterproof boots, though. Ensure they're at least knee height for wet landings and ideally have soles with a good grip for scrambling over rocks and ice, and picking your way around colonies of chinstrap penguins.

Packing essentials

- Parka life: most Antarctic ships provide a take-home parka jacket to each passenger (you'd hope so, given the astronomical fares associated with such voyages), so leave that hulking great down-filled puffer jacket at home.
- Chill out: Antarctic cruising is generally casual, so you don't need that ball gown. Each operator has different dress codes and supplied kit, however, so read up before you travel. Once you're south of the departure ports, you'll find plenty of elephant seals but not many boutiques.
- Best bins: pack the highest-spec pair of binoculars you can afford, and a camera with a good zoom, unless you want to see nothing but the occasional finned blob.

Pack for pong

If you've got a sensitive nose or stomach, be aware that penguin colonies are stinky places to visit, especially in February when chicks begin their moult. A judiciously placed scarf can help ease the olfactory offensive, and will be a welcome extra layer when back on board a ship that's being buffeted around in rough seas.

Case study: Antarctica

Pack a sense of wilderness wonder. This grand icy continent, accessible only from November to March, has no towns, no villages, no nothing, apart from the occasional research station. Embrace the elements, but also protect yourself against them. Contact lenses dry out in harsh wind, so pack glasses. Even without sunshine, reflected glare from the elements can burn, so bring creams. And pack a back-up camera or spare battery; the latter drain in cold weather and shutters become temperamental.

Antarctic cruise departure hub Ushuaia is a good base from which to explore the lakes, valleys and forests of the Parque Nacional Tierra del Fuego. If you choose to do so, pack smart: hiking boots and quick-drying trekking trousers are invaluable.

Where are you going? The Poles

Arctic

When packing for the Arctic, consider which side of the Gulf Stream you're travelling to. Air temperatures at 70°N in Scandinavia are much milder than other parts at the same latitude (we're looking at you, frigid Canada). That said, you're not going to be basking in the sun anywhere – just the beauty of the Northern Lights, if you're lucky. If you're keen on capturing beautiful aurora borealis photos, consider packing a good camera and tripod.

Trips to the Arctic are active, demanding technical kit and clothing. Tour operators usually supply the essentials, so cut back on expense and space accordingly. Unless you're going to visit the region repeated times and want your own kit, don't splash out on specialist stuff you'll probably never use again.

Packing essentials

- Wear wool: there's a reason that the Sami favour wool and fur; natural fibres offer supreme warmth in this climate. Woollen socks, if nothing else, are a must.
- Active underwear: snowshoeing, cross-country skiing, husky-sledding – trips to this part of the world are action-packed, so ensure your base layers are high-wicking or you'll freeze.
- Outer calm: jackets should be the thickest layer and both windproof and waterproof, with a hood. Many Arctic tour operators provide boiler suits for outdoor activities, so you might not need to invest in a full ski suit.

Clothing that communicates
Gakti, the traditional dress of the Sami, features patterns that signify status and family. So, when you bag that souvenir scarf, ask what it spells out...

Case study: Finnish Arctic
You're not likely to have experienced such cold before – or such a level of outdoor activity in conditions in which your face freezes but your body boils. Banish cotton because it absorbs sweat and makes you colder. High-wicking base layers of wool or synthetics are best.

Bring cream for dry skin (don't apply it less than 30 minutes before heading out or it'll freeze pores solid). Thin inner gloves under mitts are finger-savers when negotiating cameras and zips.

© Frozenmost / Getty Images

Where are you going? Desert
Luxury desert camping

From the Australian Outback and the red dunes of Dubai to the subtropical sands of Namibia and India, the desert can be a well-managed wilderness for the modern traveller. Where once was nought but sands and camels, and the sort of endless dunes that almost did for pioneering explorers such as Wilfred Thesiger, now stand luxury camps and wadi-bashing 4WD tours. These seas of silica are even the stuff honeymoons are made of, a *One Thousand and One Nights'* fantasy made real in opulent Bedouin tents lit by candle and starlight. Like a Khalifa, you will want for nothing, and prudent packing will protect you from the elements.

Packing essentials
- Hang loose: choose light-coloured (sun-reflecting) loose-fitting clothing – lightweight but not sun-penetrable shirts with collars, and trousers that allow skin to breathe and limbs to move freely when negotiating jeeps and camels.
- Headcase: bandanas, hats, scarves are all essentials, offering protection against sun, sand and wind. They also add welcome layers when those fearsome rays sink beneath the horizon.
- Shoe sense: breathable trainers or lightweight hiking boots will protect toes from hot midday sands and chilly desert nights. A smart pair of (flat) sandals will provide glamour and footloose freedom at other times.

Case study: Gobi Desert

The go-to destination for high-end wilderness explorers. Whether you choose a fixed lodge-style camp or stay in a traditional ger (portable round tent) with a host family, you'll still need to be prepared for harsh extremes of climate. Here, winds from the Siberian Steppe rattle across exposed rock, with day and night temperatures fluctuating as much as 35°C.

A windproof jacket or shell and liner are a must, as is some sort of head covering, along with a bandana to protect your neck and face when the wind whips up. A smart scarf adds a certain panache. And pack gear suitable for horseback. It's said that a Mongol without a horse is like a bird without wings, and no good camp's complete without horses. You don't want to be in tight trousers…

Omani etiquette

This welcoming desert country is deeply conservative. Ripped jeans, suspect slogans or risqué images will not be well regarded in rural areas. Dress modestly, wherever you stay.

Where are you going? Desert
High-desert trekking

 From the Great Basin and the Mojave deserts of the USA to the Sahara-backed Moroccan Atlas Mountains, take a high-altitude desert trek and it soon becomes clear that not all deserts are made of sand. Packing for active trips here needs to take temperature extremes into account, along with footwear and kit that can tackle rough, rocky, exposed terrain. Take a leathery leaf out of a cowboy's book and stay covered up. The more skin is exposed to the elements, the more evaporation (and dehydration) occurs.

Packing essentials

- Be bio: you will probably be travelling through some pristine, if not protected areas, so pack your toiletry bag accordingly. Go for biodegradable soaps and lotions where possible and, if you want to up your chances of spotting wildlife, ditch scented deodorants and perfumes.
- Let there be light: the sun will be beating you into submission all day, but once it's gone, you'll be left wanting its illumination. Pack a headtorch and a spare, for ease of hands-free navigation.
- Go solar: in these sun-soaked parts of the world, a solar charger will get more than enough exposure to be useful. That said, Wi-Fi and phone signals are likely to be scant, so while your devices may be charged, their use will be limited. Consider a GPS as a back-up, and perhaps a traditional compass, too.

Ice and spice

In Morocco, where the Sahara is backed by the arid, often snow-capped Atlas Mountains, you will need more than shorts and T-shirts. Pack a couple of longer layers and at least one thick outer – a fleece jumper is a cosy solution that takes up minimal space when not being worn, as is a micro-fibre down jacket.

Case study: Atacama Desert

This is one of the driest places on earth: your packing mission here is to keep covered and hydrated. The gateway town of San Pedro de Atacama sits just above the threshold for altitude sickness. And from here on, it continues going up. Carry a daypack with plenty of water and you should acclimatise. In case you don't, pack some Diamox.

Where are you going? Safari
Big-Five country

 The tiny charter plane that delivers you deep into the African bush dictates all when it comes to suitcase strategy. For over-packers, the associated weight restrictions are as brutal as a lion kill – limiting you to luggage that averages as little as 10kg. And within this small soft duffle (forget wheelie cases) you need to combine kit that is functional, photogenic and, ideally, includes some outfits that have at least a little Karen Blixen/Denys Finch Hatton-esque fashion flair (cashmere and silk along with the ubiquitous fleece).

Packing essentials
- Colour me glad: up your chances of getting nose to whisker with the big game and blend in with the bush by wearing natural, earthy tones. Solids, darks, whites and brights are out.
- Get protective: thicker clothing is a good defence against insects but it's wearying to wear in the heat. Buy a couple of choice pieces of clothing that are UV-protective and pre-treated with bug repellent.
- Camera kit and caboodle: powerful binoculars, a compact camera for snaps, SLR and long-range lenses, extra batteries, memory cards, charger… Photographic gear will already account for much of your luggage, but it's worth considering an additional item: a rubber air-blower to remove grit and sand from clogged cameras and lenses – an easy featherweight fix.

Banish the biting blues
Where the tsetse fly is at large, avoid wearing blue or bright clothing, which attract the bug. Tsetse flies can spread sleeping sickness.

Case study: Serengeti
This is one of the rare places where you should splurge on that hotel service wash. With luggage restrictions on local planes and laundry services as standard in most safari lodges, you can cut your clothing requirements in half by laundering – and ever-present savannah dust means you'd probably need to, regardless of how much spare clothing you've managed to cram in.

A waterproof bag? In the African plains? Yes: essential to protect kit from sudden downpours but more useful for defending valuables against that dust.

A tablet is a boon in the bush. It can squirrel away wildlife guides, back up photos and illuminate evenings with apps that map the stars, light your tent and identify that obscure bird call.

© Hannes Thirion /Getty Images

Where are you going? Safari
Beyond the Big Five

When we think of safari we imagine hot savannah and tinderbox-dry, lion-patrolled bush. But in the watery Okavango Delta, the Atlantic-backed landscapes of Namibia and the lush forests of northern Kenya and Rwanda, there are just as many unique wildlife wonders to be seen – gorillas, baboons, chimpanzees, crocs and prolific birdlife. Here, your kit will need to accommodate humid, wet and often steep terrain. As a rule: pack light and wear your bulkier items when in transit.

Packing essentials

- Happy feet: swap muddy, hot boots at the end of the day for flip-flops (choose these rather than fancy leather sandals because you'll probably be in conditions that don't necessarily stay dry). Lodges are generally laid-back places, so two pairs of shoes will be sufficient.
- Sporty smalls: with hot, humid conditions, it's advisable to separate active daywear undies from the rest of your luggage. Wicking shirts and sports bras come in handy (the latter, especially on bumpy game drives), and can be aired overnight.
- Early-start solutions: a pack of wet wipes (dispose responsibly) and some leave-in/dry shampoo are good for early mornings when there's no time for a shower. As is a headtorch, because wildlife-watching often starts before dawn.

Case study: Rwanda

People come for those gorillas in the mist but leave with enduring memories of heart-warming encounters with villagers, wild volcanic vistas and dense forest. But with remote often comes rudimentary. Pack a repellent-treated mozzie net in case your lodge is lacking. Use a duffle with padded harness straps that can also be carried like a backpack.

They may be made in Canada, but the Tilley is the go-to headwear for African-wildlife lovers, a hardwearing hemp hat that's perfect in humidity. For feet, choose sturdy walking shoes that are closed-toe and waterproof. And pack your swimwear. Unlike many African bodies of water, Rwanda's freshwater Lake Kivu is free from crocs and hippos – a hub for watery R&R.

Kikoy **joy**
A cotton *kikoy* is east Africa's traditional blanket/wrap/scarf solution. Choose one in muted colours for wildlife-watching.

© Eric Lafforge

Where are you going? Camping
Die-hard camping fans

 The weather, terrain and time of year matter not. Have tent, will camp. The aim is to get as far away from an A-road as possible and commune with nature, albeit muddy or bug-filled. Sleeping under the stars is a seductive idea, but basic camping still needs some preparation. For example, even if you're not doing the whole camping-stove bit, you might consider a compact jetboiler. The bare minimum for self-sufficiency is a pocket knife with a bottle opener and scissors. And perhaps a spork (you guessed it, a spoon/fork combo). Choose things that have multiple functions, such as a torch lantern.

Packing essentials
- Big it up: go for a tent with a larger berth than the number of people sleeping in it, to leave space for luggage and sanity.
- Pack spares: carry extra tent pegs (you *will* bend one out of functional shape), duct tape for rips and draughts, and at least one more layer than you think you'll need, including for legs. If you've been hiking all day, those muscles will want keeping warm or they'll seize up. And even if you haven't been hard at it, long johns or cosy over-wear mean campfire sessions can last that bit longer.
- Sleep snug: pack a little beanie to wear in bed and/or bring a sleeping bag with a hood. If you're too cold to sleep through the night, daylight hours will be as miserable as those you've passed tossing and turning.

Bear proof packing
Camping in backcountry
North America? Pack pepper
spray to fend off bears. Don't
sleep in the clothes you
cooked in and lock food away
in a container strung a few
metres from the floor.

Case study: Wales
Those brooding Black Mountains and ironed-flat Brecon Beacons,
the wild coast… The rain. Oh, yes: the rain. And the wind. Atlantic-
facing, this corner of the British Isles is doubtless one of the most
beautiful but it's also an elemental place. Campers should pack for
all four seasons, regardless of your month of travel.

When it comes to clothing, you'll need layers. Thermals are
never a bad idea, year-round, as they will at least be useful at night.
Rubber boots are de rigueur, as is a decent waterproof/windproof
jacket. With all this dour kit, you might want to jolly things up a bit.
Even if you're not camping on the gusty coast, a windbreak or little
collapsible gazebo ensures privacy and weather protection – and
may mean you don't have to retreat inside the tent quite so hastily.

Where are you going? Camping
Fair-weather glampers

 What constitutes a tent in the world of glamping would make Lord Baden-Powell turn in his grave. Far from the canvas A-frame simplicity of early Scouting (and even further from a nylon one-man), 'tents' today are often architecturally glorious, semi-permanent structures. Whether you bed down in a safari-style wooden 'tent' in Spain, sleep up above the Californian redwoods in a 'floating' tree tent, or commune with your inner nomad in a yurt in Scotland,

it's likely your lodgings will come with plush bedding, a wood burner and freshly laid eggs. As you won't need to pack for substance here, pack for style instead.

Packing essentials

- **Pretty it up:** with no need to fill cases and the car with roll mats and a tent, you can indulge in such space-hogging luxuries as a wide-brimmed sun hat, that Cath Kidston picnic blanket/tea towel and, but of course, a portable espresso-maker.

- **Nurture not nature:** your carefully curated camping surroundings shouldn't leave you too exposed, but should you feel vulnerable (read: smell/hear the farm life), add some glamour with a Jo Malone travel candle and a retro Bluetooth speaker.

- **Camping cook-off:** you simply must make use of all the locally-sourced farm goodies laid on, not to mention the berries and mushrooms the children have dutifully foraged. So ensure you pack the latest cookbook.

An island of one's own
Sweden and Finland excel
at private-island retreats
where you can canoe, swim
and camp in solitude. Even
the most basic Swedish
campsites usually provide
loos, shelter and firewood, so
while glampsites might enjoy
minimalist design, they're
fully kitted out. Use the space
saved on beds and linen for
super-size cans of bug spray.

Case study: France
Tipis, yurts, safari and bell
tents, gypsy caravans and
artfully-designed tree houses:
France is full of these things.

For better-guaranteed sun
and a laid-back vibe, head to
the south Atlantic or Med
coasts, where seafood is fresh
and wine is cheap. The joy of
these sites is that most of the
big stuff – the tent, along with
beds and linen – is supplied.

Aim to use biodegradable
toiletries, as you're likely to be
staying in or near conservation
areas. Bring a little brush to
sweep out sandy/dusty floors
and keep your posh tent
sitting pretty.

© Lottie Davies

Where are you going? Round the world (RTW)
RTW: female travellers

Women's packing requirements are more complex than men's for a trip like this. First off: choose the wrong backpack and you're in for a world of back pain. Get one properly sized and fitted at a travel shop and ensure it spreads the weight across your hips, taking the strain off your back. When you're shouldering the thing for several hours, walking through that truck blockade in Bolivia, you'll be thankful. And keep in mind that the world is not as savage as you think. You don't need to pack your entire home into a bag to survive.

Packing essentials

- **Hair-brained:** you do not need that hairdryer/-curler/-straightener. It will weigh you down more than it perks up your locks. A small quick-drying towel and plenty of hairbands, for long hair, will suffice.
- **Shoe-in:** for this type of trip, four pairs will be your absolute limit and should include: comfy everyday walking shoes/sandals (let climate dictate); a pair of flip-flops for beach/hostel showers; decent hiking boots/shoes if your trip calls for it; and finally some smart footwear – choose lightweight flats over heels. If you find yourself really stuck for stacked smarts, a cheap pair can be bought en route.
- **Menstrual matters:** towels and tampons can be purchased pretty much everywhere these days, but it's good to have a small pouch for emergencies, including pain meds.

LBD dahling
There's a reason why seasoned RTW female travellers list the little black dress as their 'never travels without' item. It's so versatile: dress it up or down to navigate any social situation.

Pack light
In order to enjoy the world, you want to be light on your feet. This is essential for anyone who wants to embrace the beautiful chaos of travel – and to remain as independent as possible. Want to run for that imminently departing Shinkansen train in Japan without causing titters of embarrassment? Need to cram on to an Indian bus without your bag forcing you to sit in someone's lap? Want to gamely leap into that Thai fishing boat without having to get the captain and all his mates to help you aboard? Then pack light. As a starting point, choose a bag that easily fits into the overhead locker of a plane cabin but also has the capacity to expand. And here's the best rule: if clothing takes up more than half the space, you're probably taking too much.

Where are you going? Round the world (RTW)

RTW: male and female travellers

 How to fit kit for two hemispheres into one bag? Doing so is the key to packing successfully for a true RTW. There is, sadly, no cut-and-dried solution, but as a starting point, consider what you can ditch as much as what's essential. If you need heavy trekking boots and a down jacket in New Zealand or South America at the start but won't use them again as you travel via the South Pacific/Asia, consider sending stuff home as it becomes redundant.

Packing essentials

- Pull the cord: you can use a bungee or parachute cord to tie things to the outside of your pack, make a line to dry clothes, or strap your bag to the roof of a bus. Taking one will also make you feel a bit Bond.
- Plug it: does your room-mate snore like a howler monkey? Pack earplugs. These will also serve you well when bedding down in Changi for that long airport layover, on that mariachi music-playing Mexican bus after one too many tequilas, or during that clattering long-distance Indian train journey. Feeling more sharing? Pack a headphone-splitter so you and your travel companion can watch the same movie together.
- Travel trilogy: the lucky formula for light packers comes in threes. Namely three pairs of socks, three pairs of underwear and three shirts; one to wear, one to wash, one to dry. You get more miles out of legwear, so two items will do.

Frisbee friends

A frisbee may not seem like essential kit, but visit any beach/park, whip it out and marvel at its friend-making prowess. It can also act as a plate, bottle-opener, fan and dry place to sit.

Go with the flow

Considering climate is key to successful packing for a RTW trip. Not everyone likes to chase summer around the world, but it does make for lighter/easier packing. So consider choosing your global route so that it follows the seasons in some sort of logical progression, enabling you to buy/ditch layers as you go.

Unlike shorter trips, there's more downtime on a RTW, so you can launder clothes, and what wears out, gets lost or you find lacking can usually be purchased for very little.

Live by layers. These pack down, can be removed or added and, unless you're hiking the Andes or doing winter sports, a windproof/waterproof outer with several layers underneath should keep you just as toasty as a bulky winter coat would.

Where are you going? Action
Soft adventure

Inn-to-inn walking and dining in France or birding in Tobago? Soft adventure trips give you an in on local culture and nature but require little prior experience or skill. Most of the specialist kit required is usually provided by your tour operator, leaving you free to pack the frills that ensure convenient and comfortable travels. That sleek pair of binoculars, specialist guidebook or outfit for evening wine tasting can be added to the packing list.

Packing essentials

- Russian dolls: having several bags that fit inside one another and into your main bag is a great way to contain wet kit, separate out specialist clothing and squirrel away souvenirs. Soft adventure trips often involve diverse activities, so each day's needs may be quite different. Sometimes a dry bag will serve you better than a standard daypack. Either way, 20–40L is the optimum capacity.
- Self-soothing: the level of activity may involve little risk, but you're still likely to pick up some scrapes and blisters. Bare minimum first-aid kit: plasters (band-aids)/second skin, some arnica cream, ibuprofen, antiseptic cream.
- Transfer tedium: multi-activity trips can involve lengthy (and boring) road transits between destinations. This is where a phone stocked with music and audiobooks, or a tablet loaded with that latest TV box set, really come into their own.

Sea fun in St Lucia

Stand-up paddle boarding and Snuba diving can both be enjoyed in St Lucia with no prior experience (the latter involves a surface air supply rather than the regulator and tank of its cousin Scuba). You'll be spending a lot of time getting in and out of the water, so it's worth packing a rash vest rather than just relying on sun cream.

Case study: cycling in Italy

Freewheel along the scenic roads that line the Trentino-Alto Adige, bronze the legs on the *Ciclopista del Sole*, and coast the lakeshore coasts of Garda: a classic two-wheeled soft adventure.

Consider padded bike shorts, along with gloves. Both will cushion skin but the latter will also improve grip when hands get sweaty. Select breathable, fingerless ones for summer. You don't need specialist cycling shoes; multi-activity shoes are fine.

Organised inn-to-inn tours usually transport your luggage ahead of you or supply panniers. A bum, hip or courier bag is more ergonomic than a backpack for your daily needs. Serious bikers may want to take their own pedals, but beware: carriage fees and new packaging rules can make this process pricey and painful.

Where are you going? Action
Hard-core adventure

 Whether you're overlanding in Iceland's volcanic landscapes, long-distance hiking and white-water rafting in Canada's wild west or kayaking along the high-altitude Zanskar River in Ladakh, hard adventure travel is pretty much guaranteed to involve an intimate experience with the natural environment. The weather and where you sleep is of little concern; the adventure must go on. So pack for self-sufficiency. Travel with special meds? If you're going to be miles from anybody who speaks your language, it's always best to carry a prescription written in generic, chemical form rather than brand names.

Packing essentials
- Navigation and illumination: map; compass; GPS; headtorch; spare batteries and bulbs; if camping, three fire-lighting tools: lighter, matches and tinder.
- Repair and shelter: basic first-aid kit, tailored to the demands of your destination and activity; multi-tool knife; duct tape; dental floss (doubles as strong thread) plus needle and thread; spare blanket and/or a poncho that can double as a rain shelter.
- Insulation: a set of silk or merino-wool long johns and vest that packs down to nothing; a warm hat; a sarong/scarf. It's a myth that we lose most body heat from our heads, but the face, head and chest are more sensitive to temperature changes than the rest of the body, so require more protection.

Chinese waters
Even if you haven't climbed before, you'll want to scale the limestone karst peaks of Yangshuo in southern China, which has Asia's best concentration of climbs for all abilities. You'll build up a thirst, but only go for brand-name bottled water; cheap filtered and tap water/ice are a no-no. Take Imodium Chews and a bottle of Pepto-Bismol.

Case study: New Zealand
A trip through New Zealand can be like visiting several countries with different climates. Hiking along a Pacific beach, paddling a white-water river and climbing a glacier in one day is entirely possible (with a bungee jump thrown in, of course). An ideal jacket will be something that is warm and waterproof, but won't leave you drenched in sweat should the temperature or activity level rise. Choose something with a shell and inner fleece layer that can either be worn alone or together, meaning it will be adaptable.

Follow the cardinal cotton rule of active travel: cotton can kill the experience if it gets wet and cold. Choose synthetic or merino wool clothing you can layer. Pack clothing/daypacks with plenty of pockets for easy access to your gear while you're in action.

Packing lists

Top tips

From city and beach to pistes and wilderness, here are some of our favourite travel life hacks.

City

- The capsule wardrobe comes into its own for a city break: one skirt or pair of trousers can be teamed with multiple tops in complementary colours.

- A pair of trainers will be vital for covering acres of pavement over many hours. Make sure you stow a pair of killer heels or brogues in your bag to slip on when you're just around the corner from that great restaurant.

- Layers will regulate the chills or the heat when you're on the street. Choose something that can look dressy amid those layers in case you need to spruce up at a moment's notice. A collar peeping out amid the woollies, for example, can help you look smart.

- Natural fibres will keep you more comfortable as you move between different temperatures, from gallery space to local park.

- Come rain or shine, take your sunglasses for a touch of style.

- A cross-body bag is a handy and secure item to use while exploring the city and will keep your belongings safe. Want to keep a tighter hold on them? Choose a clutch bag and, if it has a strap, wrap that around your wrist. Wear daypacks on your front, not your back – not a great look, but it will keep the pickpockets at bay.

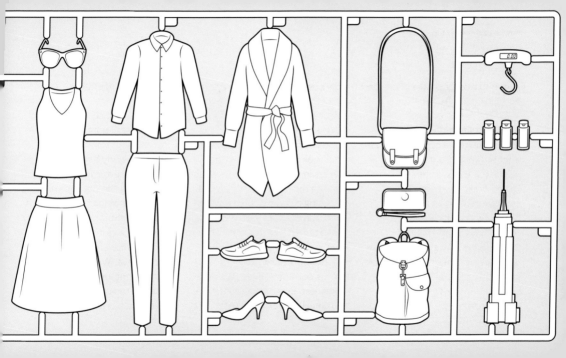

• Pop down to the local pound/dollar store to buy 100mL containers into which you can decant your favourite liquids, gels and creams. Try a roll-on perfume rather than risk smashing your favourite atomiser.

• Don't forget to weigh your suitcase before you leave home. Bust your cabin luggage allowance and you'll be hit in the wallet or even have to dump some of your belongings in the nearest bin.

Winter sports

• Don't forget your sunscreen. It may be cold, but that sun is fierce when reflected off bright white snow. Slap on some lip balm, too.

• Pack a handy cloth for wiping your goggles – and brow – on the go.

• Switch that Rolex for a cheap watch when you're on the slopes.

• Lightweight waterproof boots are a blessing for an après-ski bar crawl.

• Touchscreen-capable inner gloves will keep you connected to your technology without freezing.

• Don't forget your swimwear in case your lodgings have a hot tub.

• Invest in a helmet camera so you can impress (bore) your friends later with footage of your derring-do.

• Purchase a ski or snowboard bag with wheels to take the strain – you'll be especially thankful on the journey home.

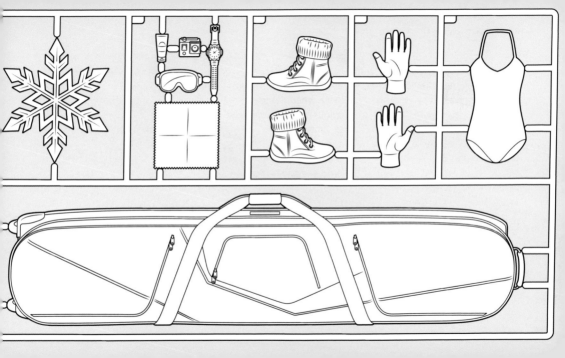

Beach

• Avoid struggling into your wetsuit by putting plastic bags on your hands and feet so you can slip it on more easily.

• Do you really need to squeeze a beach towel in your suitcase? A sarong is just as good for drying as for wearing.

• A telescopic umbrella is easy to carry and could provide relief from the sun on a deserted cove with little shade.

• Forgot the bucket and spade? That takeaway coffee cup and spoon will keep your pint-size builders busy.

• In-ear headphones are small, light and a less sweaty proposition under the burning sun. Get the sports variety that hook over your ear so they don't drop out and fall in the sand.

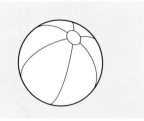

Camping/wilderness

• Just the two of you going on a camping trip? For comfort, opt for a four-berth tent.

• Pitch your tent at home before your trip – to sort out problems before you hit the road.

• Women heading off the beaten track may rue the day they laughed at the idea of buying a Shewee…

• Stand your muddy boots in a plastic bag so that you can keep them in your tent, away from the morning dew.

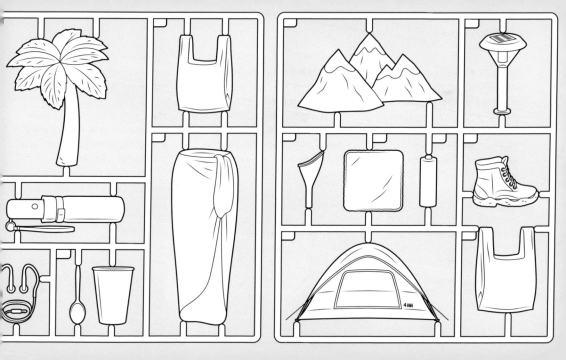

- You're unlikely to bump into a housekeeper with a fresh fluffy towel out in the wilds. Invest in a microfibre one – they're lightweight and have an insatiable thirst for water.

- Is it a little cold halfway up that mountain? Keep your batteries snug at the bottom of your sleeping bag to stop them draining.

- Solar garden lights are useful for lighting the way at night.

Family
- Some items are easier bought (and left for the next family) at your destination, such as inflatable beach toys.

- Pack a spare outfit for children in your hand luggage in readiness for those accidents.

- A cheap new toy is a great diversion when produced at the start of a long-haul flight. Or wrap up a few inexpensive ones and drip-feed them to the kids over the interminable hours.

- Want a stress-free holiday? Then don't forget your little one's favourite toy/fluffy animal/book.

- Make sure you pack a camera for the kids – they'll love it and you'll love their quirky take on the world.

- Consider packing an extension lead for charging all electronics (and avoiding arguments).

- An e-reader with a backlight is a great thing for insomniacs sharing a hotel room with the whole brood.

Packing bundles

Even short trips require precision planning. This bundle approach allows you to take a general overview of your needs before getting stuck into the detail. These packing lists cover most eventualities.

How to use these lists
Assess which bundles you'll be needing. Most trips, long or short, will need items from bundles 1 – 11. Longer trips, specialist activities and family travel are catered for in bundles 12 – 18.

Scale the bundles according to the type of trip and add in specialist kit as necessary.

BUNDLE 1: Handbag/manbag
- Mobile phone
- Keys
- Wallet/purse
- E-reader/book
- Earplugs
- Sleeping mask
- Sleeping pills/essential medication
- Notepad and pen
- Travel locks and keys
- Luggage tags
- Lightweight warm top/shawl
- Soft collapsible bag
- Umbrella
- Travel pillow

BUNDLE 2: Money and important documents
- Cash
- ATM and credit cards
- Money belt
- Passport and visas (plus copies)
- Driving licence and car insurance documents (plus copies)
- Maps, directions and itineraries

- Tickets/booking confirmations
- Emergency numbers for personal contacts, insurer and credit/debit card companies
- Medical cards and prescriptions

BUNDLE 3: Basic clothes
- Underwear
- Socks/tights/stockings
- Pyjamas

BUNDLE 4: Casual clothes
- T-shirts
- Hoodies
- Shorts
- Jeans/jogging pants
- Skirts
- Dresses

BUNDLE 5: Smart clothes
- Shirts/blouses
- Jumpers/cardigans
- Trousers
- Skirts
- Dresses
- Suits

BUNDLE 6: Outerwear
- Fleece
- Shawl/poncho
- Jackets
- Raincoats
- Hats
- Gloves
- Scarves

BUNDLE 7: Fitness
- Sportswear
- Swimwear and goggles

BUNDLE 8: Footwear
- Trainers
- Sandals
- Flip-flops
- Dress shoes
- Slippers

BUNDLE 9: Accessories
- Belts
- Ties
- Watches
- Jewellery
- Glasses and case
- Sunglasses and case

BUNDLE 10: Hygiene

- Toothbrush, toothpaste, dental floss, mouthwash
- Soap, shampoo, conditioner, flannel
- Deodorant
- Brush/comb
- Hairdryer/tongs
- Hair-styling products
- Hair accessories
- Mirror
- Cleanser
- Moisturiser
- Lip balm
- Perfume
- Make-up
- Cotton balls and buds
- Pocket tissues

- Sunscreen
- After-sun/aloe vera
- Insect repellent
- Contact lenses, solutions and case
- Shaving products and razors
- Sanitary products
- Manicure set, including tweezers
- Nail polish/remover pads
- Hand wipes/antibacterial lotion
- First-aid kit
- Lint roller

BUNDLE 11: Technology

- Mobile phone and charger
- Laptop/tablet and charger
- E-reader charger
- Portable DVD player and charger/cable
- Camera, memory card and charger
- Headphones/portable speaker
- Universal adaptor
- Spare batteries
- Torch
- Binoculars
- Alarm clock
- Satnav

BUNDLE 12: Laundry

- Laundry wash and bag
- Sewing kit
- Travel iron
- Clothes pegs
- Bungee cord

BUNDLE 13: Winter sports clothing

- Helmet
- Goggles
- Boots
- Boot- and hand-warmers
- Snood/ear muffs/headband
- Woolly hat
- Balaclava
- Non-cotton thermal top and leggings
- Ski/snowboard jacket
- Ski/snowboard trousers
- Microfleece
- Ski/snowboard gloves
- Silk/merino wool inner gloves
- Ski/snowboard socks
- Ankle/knee/wrist supports
- Kneepads
- Shoe chains

BUNDLE 14: Ski and board equipment

- Skis, poles and boots or snowboard and boots
- Ski/snowboard bag
- Boot bag
- Powder ribbons
- Snowboard leash
- Wax and iron
- Ski skins
- Ski/snowboard-holder strap
- Ski/snowboard lock
- Lift pass holder
- Walkie-talkie
- Transceiver, shovel and probe
- Compass
- Altimeter
- Multi tool
- Flask
- Water bottle

BUNDLE 15: Beach

- Sunhat
- Beach bag
- Cooler bag
- Beach towel
- Sarong
- Beach mat/deckchair
- Snorkel and goggles
- Flippers
- Beach shoes
- Sun tent
- Beach toys

- Inflatables
- Water wings/rubber rings
- Parasol
- Windbreak
- Water bottle
- Dry bag
- Talcum powder

BUNDLE 16: Camping/ wilderness clothes

- Waterproof cape
- Wicking shirts/T-shirts
- Zip-off trousers
- Hiking socks
- Walking boots
- Wellies

BUNDLE 17: Camping/ wilderness equipment

- Tent
- Sleeping pad
- Sleeping bag
- Backpack cover
- Foldable chairs
- Gazebo
- Cool box/bag
- Headtorch
- Compass/GPS
- Walking pole
- Binoculars
- Utility penknife
- Camping stove
- Lighter
- Lightweight pans
- Cup, bowl, plate and utensils

- Water bottle
- Water-purification tablets
- Vacuum flask
- Washing-up bowl
- Dishcloth
- Tea towel
- Toilet paper
- Biodegradable soap
- Rubbish bags
- Rope/clothes line
- Duct tape
- Cheap doormat
- Mosquito/insect net

BUNDLE 18: Family

- Babygros
- Nappies
- Potty
- Baby wipes
- Nappy bags
- Nappy cream
- Changing mat
- Baby monitor
- Baby blanket
- Baby carrier
- Baby/toddler-proofing kit
- Bed rail
- Night light
- Baby bottles and brush
- Drinking cup
- Sterilising tablets
- Bib
- Liquid paracetamol sachets
- Teething gel
- Teething ring
- Dummy
- Toys, games, colouring pencils and paper/book, reading books
- Car/buggy sunshade
- Car booster seat
- Mosquito/insect net
- Buggy
- Child-view mirror
- Harness/child locator

Index

About the writers

Sarah Barrell is an award-winning travel writer, most recently the author of Lonely Planet's From the Source: Italy. Former travel editor at the *Independent on Sunday*, Sarah currently works as Associate Editor for *National Geographic Traveller* (UK) and writes freelance for a wide range of titles, including *BBC Good Food*, *Independent*, the *Telegraph* and *Evening Standard*. **www.sarahbarrell.com**

Sarah would like to extend thanks, as ever, to her long-suffering family for their patience, notably to daughter Ella for finally conceding that travelling light means packing 'just' four teddies. Thanks also to travel buddy Celia Brasher for her initial brainstorming and enthusiasm, and to co-author Kate Simon for her organisational expertise and speedy creativity: the Samsonite spinner of working partners.

Kate Simon is the former travel editor of the *Independent on Sunday*. She continues to write about travel for the paper as well as other major UK publications, including the *Telegraph* and *Hello!*. Kate is also the co-founder of specialist travel PR agency Traveltappers (traveltappers.co.uk).

Kate would like to thank her partner and son, Dean and Quincy Ryan, for their inspired ideas and tea-making efforts, her business partner Simone Kane for her patience, and her pal Henrietta Roussoulis for her great connections. And thanks, of course, to co-author Sarah Barrell, for making this first foray into a publication with a hard spine a joy.

Published in July 2016 by
Lonely Planet Publications Pty Ltd
ABN 36 005 607 983
www.lonelyplanet.com
ISBN 978 1 76034 075 9
© Lonely Planet 2016
Printed in China
10 9 8 7 6 5 4 3 2 1

Written by Sarah Barrell and Kate Simon

Managing Director, Publishing Piers Pickard
Associate Publisher Robin Barton
Commissioning Editor Jessica Cole
Art Direction Daniel Di Paolo
Layout Designer Johanna Lundberg
Illustrator James Provost
Print Production Larissa Frost, Nigel Longuet

Lonely Planet offices
AUSTRALIA
Level 2 & 3, 551 Swanston Street,
Carlton 3053, Victoria, Australia
Phone 03 8379 8000
Email talk2us@lonelyplanet.com.au

USA
150 Linden St, Oakland, CA 94607
Phone 510 250 6400
Email info@lonelyplanet.com

UNITED KINGDOM
240 Blackfriars Road, London SE1 8NW
Phone 020 3771 5100
Email go@lonelyplanet.co.uk